The Future of Schooling

Educating America in 2020

Bryan Goodwin
Laura Lefkowits
Carolyn Woempner
Elizabeth Hubbell

A JOINT PUBLICATION

Solution Tree | Press

Education Resource Center
University of Delaware
Newark, DE 19716-2940

T75654

P-E
G631
2011

Copyright © 2011 by Solution Tree Press

All rights reserved, including the right of reproduction of this book in whole or in part in any form.

555 North Morton Street

Bloomington, IN 47404

800.733.6786 (toll free) / 812.336.7700

FAX: 812.336.7790

email: info@solution-tree.com

solution-tree.com

Printed in the United States of America

14 13 12 11 10   1 2 3 4 5

FSC

Mixed Sources

Product group from well-managed
forests and other controlled sources

Cert no. SW-COC-002283
www.fsc.org
© 1996 Forest Stewardship Council

Library of Congress Cataloging-in-Publication Data

The future of schooling : educating America in 2020 / Bryan Goodwin ... [et al.].

p. cm.

Includes bibliographical references and index.

ISBN 978-1-935542-45-2 (trade paper) -- ISBN 978-1-935542-46-9 (library edition) 1. Education--United States--Forecasting. 2. Educational change. I. Goodwin, Bryan.

LA217.2.F89 2011

370.973'0905--dc22

2010030284

Solution Tree

Jeffrey C. Jones, CEO & President

Solution Tree Press

President: Douglas M. Rife

Publisher: Robert D. Clouse

Vice President of Production: Gretchen Knapp

Managing Production Editor: Caroline Wise

Senior Production Editor: Lesley Bolton

Proofreader: David Eisnitz

Text and Cover Designer: Orlando Angel

Acknowledgments

Scenario planning at McREL is, as it should be, a collaborative endeavor. Therefore, during the development of the scenarios in this book, as well as the methodology and data that support them, many members of the McREL staff and board participated in countless meetings and workshops to offer their individual and collective insights in an effort to ensure that this publication is of high quality and utility to its readers.

The authors would like to particularly thank McREL's board of directors, management council, and senior directors who provided initial guidance and feedback on the construction of the scenario framework and the identification of the deep causes and key features of each scenario. As each story gained form, the entire staff at McREL offered beneficial feedback on its plausibility, relevance, and potential usefulness to the field.

Table of Contents

About McREL

Based in Denver, Colorado, McREL (Mid-continent Research for Education and Learning) is a nonprofit organization dedicated to its mission of making a difference in the quality of education and learning for all through excellence in applied research, product development, and service. For more than forty years, McREL has served as the federally funded regional educational laboratory for seven states in the U.S. heartland. Today, it provides a comprehensive array of services to an international audience of educators to help them prepare students for success in tomorrow's increasingly complex society and global marketplace. To learn more, contact McREL at 1.800.781.0156 or info@mcrel.org.

About the Authors

Bryan Goodwin is the vice president of communications and marketing at McREL. He manages McREL's corporate visibility and publications, including serving as chief editor of the McREL magazine, *Changing Schools*, which is published three times annually. During his twelve years at McREL, Bryan has written numerous articles and reports translating education research into practical application for educators and policymakers, including the 2010 report *Changing the Odds for Student Success: What Matters Most*. Articles he has written and co-written have appeared in such publications as *Educational Leadership* and *School Administrator*.

Prior to joining McREL, Bryan was a high school English teacher at the Good Hope School in St. Croix, U.S. Virgin Islands; a reporter with the Virgin Islands Daily News in St. Thomas, U.S. Virgin Islands, and the Central Penn Business Journal in Harrisburg, Pennsylvania; and a writing and journalism instructor at the Penn State University campus in Middletown, Pennsylvania.

Bryan holds an MA in rhetoric and communication studies from the University of Virginia and a BA in professional writing from Baylor University in Waco, Texas.

 **Laura Lefkowits** is director of special projects for AdvancED, a school and district accreditation and improvement organization, where she provides policy and government relations support, consults with education policymakers on translating policy into practice, and supports the implementation of the scenario-planning methodology in schools and districts across the country. Laura is also president of Lefkowits Consulting, LLC, an independent consultancy providing a wide array of services to nonprofit and for-profit organizations in the areas of strategic planning, policy development, grant proposal writing, large and small group facilitation, and project development and management. Laura served as vice president of policy and planning at McREL from 2002 through 2009, during which time she was certified by the Global Business Network as a scenario planner and developed the scenario-planning approach described in this publication.

Laura has published numerous articles in journals such as *Phi Delta Kappan* and the *American School Board Journal* and provides keynote presentations to national education audiences in scenario planning, policy development, and future-focused thinking. Laura has served as an at-large member of the Denver Public Schools Board of Education, K–12 program director for the Colorado Institute of Technology (CIT), executive director of the Colorado Mathematics, Science, and Technology Education Coalition (COMSTEC), executive director of the Colorado chapter of Physicians for Social Responsibility, and assistant director of the Dartmouth-Hitchcock Arthritis Center.

Laura has a master's degree in public administration from the Graduate School of Public Affairs, University of Colorado at Denver, where she currently serves as a lecturer.

Dr. Carolyn Woempner is senior director of corporate management support at McREL. In this position, Carolyn supports McREL at the organizational level through strategic planning and optimized operational effectiveness. Carolyn also manages several large projects addressing current problems of practice, as well as conceptual, innovative projects that address broad issues in education. Carolyn has built McREL's expertise in scenario-based planning and trends impacting the future of education. She has also focused on the policy implications of these trends, writing numerous articles and policy briefs on the topic.

Carolyn has a diverse research background, including work as a population geneticist predicting genetic variability in agricultural animal populations. She holds a master's degree in genetics from Colorado State University. After shifting her focus to the field of education, she acquired a PhD in education leadership and policy studies. Prior to joining McREL, Dr. Woempner was director of operations at a Denver-area elementary school.

Elizabeth Hubbell is a lead consultant in the Curriculum & Instruction Department at McREL in Denver, Colorado. She conducts workshops and training for K–12 teachers on research-based instructional strategies and technology integration, writes curriculum models for online classes, conducts technology audits for districts, and trains district leaders in using Power Walkthrough® software. Prior to consulting for McREL, Elizabeth served as a building-level curriculum director and elementary teacher, focusing on combining 21st century learning environments with Montessori philosophies.

Elizabeth has served on the advisory board for PBS Teacher Source and has been published in several journals, including *Principal*, *Montessori Life*, and *Learning & Leading With Technology*. She is co-author of *Using Technology With Classroom Instruction That Works*. In 2003, she was one of four national finalists named for the Technology & Learning Ed Tech Leader of the Year award.

Elizabeth earned a master's degree in information and learning technologies from the University of Colorado at Denver and a bachelor's degree in early childhood education from the University of Georgia.

Preface

BY J. TIMOTHY WATERS, ED.D., PRESIDENT AND CEO OF MCREL

In 1977, Ken Olsen, the founder, president, and chairman of Digital Equipment Corporation (DEC), one of the world's leading manufacturers of mainframe computers, stated publicly that "there is no reason for any individual to have a computer in their home" (Schein, DeLisi, Kampas, & Sonduck, 2003, p. 48).

While laughable now, at the time, Olsen's observation was reasonable and informed. The smallest, cheapest "serious" computers available were the size of a pair of refrigerators and sold for more than $200,000.

Olsen had, in fact, already *seen* the future by the time he made his now-famous proclamation; he just didn't recognize it. That same year, Apple and Commodore introduced the Apple II and PET computers respectively. Yet to Olsen's way of thinking, they weren't powerful enough to really be considered computers at all; they were just toys meant for children.

Olsen's myopia cost him and his company dearly. Digital prospered for another decade (*Fortune* magazine named Olsen "America's most successful entrepreneur" in 1986), but by the late 1980s, consumers had begun to move en masse away from Digital's networked workstation computers to PCs. By the early 1990s, Digital found itself drowning in a rising tide of red ink. In 1992, Olsen was removed as president of the company he founded; six years later, most of Digital's assets were sold off to its rival, Compaq.

Olsen's story is a cautionary tale. By all accounts, he was an innovative and forward-thinking leader. Yet because he failed to envision all the possible futures of his industry, he developed a blind spot to what is arguably one of the most important innovations of the 20th century: the personal computer.

In my role as the leader of an organization that seeks to be on the cutting edge of education innovation, I often worry, What are our blind spots? I wonder what our experiences, our successes, and our expertise may keep us from seeing.

That is why, at the dawn of the 21st century, as the world was experiencing so many profound and rapid changes in the areas of economics, technology, globalization, and demographics, we at McREL asked ourselves what it would take to meet our mission of "making a difference in the quality of education and learning for all" in such challenging times. Many of us had lived through other periods of significant change, marked by such notable education events as *Brown v. Board of Education*, the passage of the very first Elementary and Secondary Education Act (ESEA) and the Individuals with Disabilities Education Act (IDEA), and the publication of *A Nation at Risk* (National Commission on Excellence in Education, 1983). Some of us had experienced Watergate, a presidential impeachment, and the outcome of a national election being determined by the Supreme Court. Others remember Dolly the cloned sheep, Bill Gates before he became a billionaire, and life before email. And yet, in spite of all the changes we had experienced, it seemed to us that the transition to a new century would require something more of educators than anything we had known before. But what?

We addressed this question first by doing what we do best: research. We invited experts to share with us their knowledge of future trends; we learned the scenario-planning methodology as a way to manage the uncertainties inherent in these trends; we wrote scenarios and shared all of these new insights with our clients and the broader education community through publication of the book *The Future of Schooling: Educating America in 2014* (McREL, 2005).

Now, as the first decade of the 21st century draws to a close, it is time to look back at our initial foray into looking ahead and assess what we have learned about the major drivers of change in the world of education. In this publication, we provide a new set of scenarios for the year 2020. We also document trend information that undergirds these scenarios, which we believe will shape the second decade of this new century.

Collectively, these scenarios ask many "what if" questions. Here are but a few of them:

- What if the current, multibillion-dollar federal investment in education succeeds in identifying and scaling up numerous innovations that transform schooling as we know it?

- What if, on the other hand, investing billions of new dollars fails to create dramatic improvements in education? Will the public continue to support public schools as we know them?

- What if online learning becomes as commonplace in the schools of tomorrow as chalkboards were in the schools of yesterday?

- What if technology allows students to proceed at their own pace along individualized pathways, measuring their progress in real time at each step of the way?

- What if the world's best teachers are able to broadcast their lessons to thousands of students each day?

Some of the questions these scenarios pose may cause discomfort. They may even challenge basic assumptions about how education is "supposed" to be delivered. Some of these potential futures may captivate and energize you; others may dishearten or frighten you. Some may do all of the above. That's the point.

The purpose of scenario planning is not to envision how we think the future *ought* to be or even how we believe it most likely *will* be. Rather, it's to look at the world from different perspectives so that we can see through our blind spots and prepare ourselves and our students for what may lie over the horizon. In the end, whether these scenarios delight, frustrate, or frighten, what matters most is that they enlighten.

We hope that this book will help jump-start thinking about and planning for the future so that when it arrives, instead of dismissing it, declaring it preposterous, or running from it, we will all prosper and thrive in it.

Introduction

We are called to be the architects of the future,
not its victims.　　　　　　　—R. BUCKMINSTER FULLER

Every day, in schools all across America, students walk in the doors relying on teachers, principals, and support staff to meet their needs. These needs are in the "here and now" and demand the utmost from the skillful educators in whom society has placed trust. The challenges of ensuring that students learn sufficient content *every day* in order to reach high academic goals, along with performing daily administrative chores (such as completing reports, taking attendance, and monitoring student safety), consume the attention of school professionals. And yet, these same professionals know that it is not for *today* that they work so hard for their students; rather, most teachers' passion is fueled by the *future* success of their students.

This book is about that future. It makes the case that thinking beyond the day-to-day responsibilities of teaching and learning is critical to the everyday success on which educators so necessarily focus; indeed, focusing on the future will make today's work, if not actually easier, certainly more successful.

A growing body of theory, supported by evidence on emerging demographic, economic, technologic, and education trends, suggests that America's educational system is on the threshold of reinvention—a reinvention necessary to maintain relevance and excellence in a future that little resembles the present (Buchen, 2004; Coates, Mahaffie, & Hines, 1997; Dychtwald, 1999; Glenn & Gordon, 2005; Hall, 2005; Howe & Strauss, 2000; Kelly, 2006; Marx, 2000; Pink, 2001; Strauss & Howe, 1997). Just as a dam resists the growing force of rising waters, America's educational system has stubbornly held to the traditional model of schooling in the presence of rising pressures for change. Unless the inevitable force of the pressures for change is handled with foresight, deliberation, and positive action, the system, like an overburdened dam, may rupture—with unanticipated and profound results—leaving those in the wake feeling surprised, uncertain, and unprepared.

In future educational systems, the traditional mental model of the school may be obsolete. No longer will students gather at a physical facility, grouped by age and passively receiving compartmentalized information from trained adults (Pink, 2001; Stevenson, 2006). Rather, parents, students, educators, businesspeople, and policymakers will require educational systems that support the needs of 21st century learners—systems that are customizable for and by the learner, comprehensive in scope, and connected to the lives and interests of students.

In education, it seems we can no longer look to the past for examples of what to expect in the future. How does one prepare for a future that looks so unlike the past? Educators must learn how to think beyond their own experiences, assumptions, and foregone conclusions to envision alternate *plausible* futures. The purpose of this book is to help readers look *beyond* education to see how a myriad of trends in demographics, technology, politics, and economics (to name a few) are likely to reshape schooling as we know it.

We might make this case by simply disgorging an overwhelming array of facts and data points. Such an approach might appeal to some, but we assume that for most readers, it would likely serve more to confuse than enlighten. Instead, we opt for a different approach: we fast-forward to the year 2020 and offer four stories, or scenarios, that describe in vivid detail how these trends we've been tracking might shape very different alternate futures for education. Through these stories, we hope to help educators plan for and prepare for an uncertain future—not only to capitalize on opportunities these changes could bring, but also to avoid the fate of Digital Equipment Corporation and other companies and organizations that failed to anticipate and plan for the future: obsolescence. It is our hope, then, that educators will be able to take away from this book new insights about how to prepare themselves and their students for the future.

In chapter 1, we offer a brief overview of the process we used to develop these scenarios. Chapter 2 consists of a summary of the key uncertainties and predetermined factors we believe will drive change in education in the near future. In chapters 3 through 6, we present four scenarios that depict how converging trends could dramatically alter the landscape of teaching and learning by 2020. Chapter 7 provides ways that educators can use the information in this book to take concrete actions to prepare themselves and their organizations for the future.

Why Scenarios?

Yogi Berra is said to have once observed that "it's tough to make predictions, especially about the future." Like most of Yogi's mangled aphorisms, there's truth in this one, too. Thus, we want to be very clear at the outset of this book that the scenarios featured herein are *not* predictions. Instead, they are stories that we believe light the way to the future. And, although the stories that follow are rooted in evidence, they are still fictional accounts of the future. What's most important about these stories is not their accuracy, but rather the extent to which they are able to help you begin to expect the unexpected and anticipate what might otherwise have been unanticipated.

Indeed, it is the interpretation and response we are after. Scenarios are meant to be plausible representations of what *could* happen if certain factors that are highly uncertain today resolve themselves in specific ways in the future. By analyzing their content and discussing their implications, scenarios become powerful tools in any organization's strategic-planning arsenal. Although they typically depict life a decade or more in the future, by using a disciplined methodology, scenarios can help individuals and organizations identify the actions they should take today to maximize their chances of success tomorrow.

So, as stated earlier, the purpose of this book is not to *predict* the future; rather, it is to stimulate a new way of thinking, sometimes known as "scenario thinking," and thus create a new kind of problem solver, the "scenario thinker." What are the characteristics of scenario thinkers? First, scenario thinkers *assume* that they live with great uncertainty. They are not deterministic. They do not see the world in black and white, nor do they make statements such as:

- ✖ "The Cold War will never end."

- ✖ "China could never threaten the United States' economic position in the world."

- ✖ "Americans will never elect a black man as president."

Second, scenario thinkers "re-perceive" reality, which involves questioning their assumptions about the way the world works so that, in the end, they see reality more clearly. Scenarios help change one's view of reality so that it matches more closely with what reality actually is and may be.

And, third, scenario thinkers are good conversationalists. Scenarios are not stand-alone documents. They are intended to be used as strategic conversation starters—not to answer questions but, rather, to raise them. Good scenario thinkers understand this, and they weave stories in such a way as to *provoke discussion* rather than to end it.

One of the most interesting aspects of becoming a scenario thinker is the new perspectives that develop when information is viewed through scenarios. News that was previously interesting in a general sense becomes highly relevant to strategic decision making when scenarios are employed. For example, in the scenarios presented in this book, information about the development and adoption of national standards becomes critical to decision making because of the impact that national standards have on possible futures. The scenario thinker sees the implications of that information beyond the short term.

Every scenario is supported by trends. Every scenario is played out through a series of "if this happens, then this could happen." Events lead from the present into the unknown future. Identifying the important trends and tracking how those trends play out is an important part of using scenarios to craft a plan of action.

By learning how to identify the signals of change in the environment as we go about daily life, we begin to understand that nothing is as certain as uncertainty. By remaining alert to indicators of change, we are less likely to be taken by surprise when actual change occurs. Trends appear everywhere once you begin to take notice—in advertisements, on TV and radio, and in fashion and music. Pay attention to what's happening at home and abroad. As author Thomas Friedman (2006) reminds us, the world is flat. A change in China will influence behavior in the United States before we know it.

Once an important trend has been identified, scenaric thinkers make a plan to collect information about that trend. By definition, a trend unfolds over time. The following hints will help you collect information about a trend so that you can put the information to use in decision making:

- Look frequently.

- Look at a variety of sources.

- Look with an open mind.

- Look over time for a prevailing theme, direction of movement, or resolution. Alternatively, look for indications that the issue will not be resolved and needs to be discarded as an important trend.

- Look at what the trend information tells you about the future and your action plan.

Scenaric thinking is a habit of mind that allows us to filter the important from the merely interesting and to understand the implications of this information in our strategic decision making.

Peter Schwartz (1991), in his seminal work on scenario planning, *The Art of the Long View*, refers to scenarios as an imaginative leap into the future. Strategic planners sometimes reject scenarios because they deem them to be too qualitative to be used as serious planning tools. Schwartz and anyone who has spent time engaged in the art and science of scenario planning would strongly disagree. In fact, scenarios are carefully researched stories, full of detail about current and emerging trends that adds credibility and brings forth new understandings that would not be possible using quantitative methodologies alone.

The point of a scenario-planning process is not to identify one of the created scenarios as the preferred future. Rather, it is to understand the likelihood that any of the created stories could in fact become reality, consider what actions we would take if such realities were to unfold, and, in this way, truly be prepared for whatever reality we encounter tomorrow, the next day, or a decade from now.

Scenarios challenge our assumptions about the future and, by doing so, lead to better decision making. When we strategize through the lens of scenarios, the future is accounted for in the decisions we make. It is this process and the ways of thinking it through that help us to develop strategies to survive and thrive during tumultuous times.

Is it difficult to become a scenaric thinker? Not at all. As humans, we are hardwired to plan ahead. You're probably familiar with the famous story about Canadian hockey player Wayne Gretzky, who remarked that when he was on the ice, his eyes didn't follow the puck's path but rather looked to where the puck was going to end up. This neurological ability to look ahead, spontaneous and intuitive on Gretzky's part, is closely tied to our innate capacity for imagination and foresight. As the skates are to the ice, so is the pen to the paper, as a scenario creates a slick description of the space between where the puck is today and where it will land in the uncertain future.

While creating these descriptions, scenaric thinkers are constantly asking, "What if?" What if the future is not the same as the past? What if the way we have always imagined things to be is not the way they will be? What then?

Exchanging ideas with people outside of our own areas of expertise is also essential. It's important to keep books and periodicals on our reading lists that are outside of our areas of expertise. (Check out the reading list in Resources to Keep the Conversation Alive, page 133, for some ideas.) Talk with people in other fields and ask them where they see the future heading.

Exploration of the Future

Writing scenarios about the future of education requires re-perceiving the future and imagining all aspects of the way the world might be, not just those factors that relate specifically to education. Indeed, the political environment, the economy, security issues, technological innovations, and social values will all impact and contribute to the unfolding of the future of education. We began our own exploration of the future in 2003 by inviting various experts to McREL to share their knowledge and insights about trends in their specialty areas.

We learned from Glen Hiemstra, founder of Futurist.com, about the potential for radical anti-aging techniques, genetic therapies, nanotechnology, and changes in the nature of work and retirement. Chris Dede, from the Harvard Graduate School of Education, exposed us to concepts of "ubiquitous learning," and noted educational demographer Harold (Bud) Hodgkinson taught us about the impact of major demographic changes (aging, racial diversity, immigration) on our future lifestyles, workplaces, schools, and other public institutions.

Neil Howe, historian, economist, and demographer, shared with us the characteristics and historical impact of different generations, as well as the different leadership styles we might expect as Baby Boomers retire. Jack Jennings, from the Center on Education Policy in Washington, DC, and a former subcommittee staff director and general counsel for the U.S. House of Representatives' Committee on Education and Labor, provided a glimpse into the future of education policy and the No Child Left Behind (NCLB) Act of 2001, in particular. Finally, we learned about the economic impacts of consumer behavior and the "Great Winter" forecasted by the Harry S. Dent Foundation from its president, Rodney Johnson.

These experts provided the inspiration for us to begin a disciplined approach to discovering trends of the future in many different areas. We began to archive these trends in a matrix that shows the interaction between various key institutions and drivers of change: homes and lifestyles, jobs and workplaces, government and policy, and education and schools. Today, we identify articles in the daily press and in professional journals and categorize them based on what they tell us about how different drivers, such as technology, economics, demographics, and globalization, are likely to impact any or all of these institutions. As we build the archive, we are constantly reminded of the many ways in which forces that are beyond our control may have an impact on the future of education. At the same time, we draw inferences from this information and incorporate those insights into our ongoing strategic-planning process.

A Look Ahead to 2020

Though the principles upon which we use scenario-planning tools to anticipate the future have not changed, the world is a very different place from the one we wrote of in 2005. At that time, the charter school movement was just beginning to be a driving force for change in American schools. Today, charter schools are so mainstream as to have become part of the U.S. Department of Education's reform strategy (U.S. Department of Education, Office of Elementary and Secondary Education, 2009). In 2005, there were concerns about the "privatization" of education and whether corporate interests such as Microsoft, Dell, or Edison might actually take over enough schools to shift control of schooling toward the private sector. Today, corporations seem to have lost interest (read: *profits*) in actually running traditional schools and are instead looking for other ways to have an impact, such as through the delivery of instructional programs online.

As the world has changed, so have the scenarios we use to chart our course into the future. Over the past several years, we have built our expertise in gathering and analyzing trend data. We have worked with numerous organizations across the country to help them write their own scenarios for the future and to create action plans from them.

There is evidence all around us that we have been using outmoded ways of thinking—in our economy, in politics, and in education. At McREL, however, we believe that scenaric thinking will help us to change, to imagine, to ask "what if," and to consider futures that are unlike the past. In this way, we can prepare for whatever future unfolds. With creative foresight and careful planning, we expect to continue to successfully impact teaching and learning for decades to come.

To state the obvious, the future will come. The only question is, will we be prepared to survive and thrive in the future, or will we become obsolete and irrelevant in the new world? We choose to be prepared and hope you will join us.

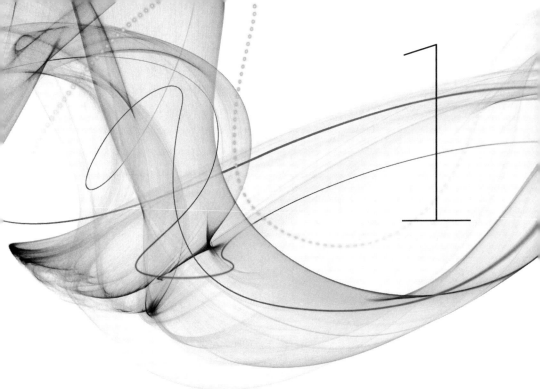

Welcome to 2020

In the early 1970s, top executives at Royal Dutch Shell had an uneasy feeling that their world was about to change, profoundly and forever. As Art Kleiner recounts in his book *The Age of Heretics: A History of the Radical Thinkers Who Reinvented Corporate Management* (2008), as the seventies dawned, nations of the Organization of Petroleum Exporting Countries (OPEC) were expressing growing discontent about simply renting their land to oil companies; they now wanted a piece of the action—namely, stock in the oil companies. At the same time that these dark clouds were forming over the oil supply, global thirst for oil continued to rise, putting the world only one or two oil-supply hiccups away from a major spike in prices.

Shell executives could see that these two trends were on a collision course—one that could lead to a worldwide oil shortage and economic calamity. Shell officials and managers knew they needed to do something different, yet they weren't sure what course to take. So, for the most part, they proceeded with business as usual—buying the same equipment, leases, and contracts as if nothing would happen.

A team of twenty forward-thinking executives at Shell, however, began to plot a different course. They gathered all the information they could find about the "triangle" of the three key players in the world's energy economy: oil companies, oil-producing nations, and oil-consuming nations. They began role-playing how these three players might respond to key predetermined events, inevitable occurrences such as the continued rising global demand for oil, which they viewed as being as predictable as heavy rains in the mountains creating floods a few days later in downstream villages.

Eventually, these forward thinkers wrote six stories about what might happen over the next few years and how the key players in the oil economy might respond to various predetermined events. Five of the scenarios painted more or less rosy pictures of the future (with optimistic titles like "Surprise-Free World" and "Three Miracles"). In these five scenarios, free-market forces or expanded drilling in Western countries were expected to save the day—the prevailing view at the time within the industry. One scenario, however, painted a darker picture. It envisioned, among other occurrences, an Iran where a growing population, declining oil reserves, and concerns about fundamentalist Islamic revolution would prompt the shah, the erstwhile friend of the oil companies, to reluctantly raise prices. On the heels of the shah's decision, other oil-producing countries—especially those less favorably inclined to the West—would quickly fall in line, cutting production and raising prices.

It was a scenario that most Shell executives did not want to hear or think about. Yet they intuitively sensed its plausibility. Slowly at first, then more systematically, managers throughout the company began to justify their decisions based on the six scenarios—including the crisis one. While their competitors continued to ignore the changes occurring around them and conduct business as usual, the executives at Shell began to make different decisions about where to drill and what kind of oil leases to make. Shell managers became more frugal, bracing the company for the worst-case scenario.

In October 1973, that scenario did occur. In response to U.S. support for Israel during the so-called Yom Kippur war, the Arab members of OPEC imposed an embargo, sharply cutting exports and raising prices. Of all the major oil companies, then called the "seven sisters" of oil, Royal Dutch Shell (which had once been labeled the "ugly sister" for its small stature among its rivals) was much better prepared than its competitors and eventually went from being the ugly sister of the industry to the main competitor of the world's largest oil company, Exxon (Schwartz, 1991). By anticipating the future, Shell was able to position itself not only to ride out the crisis, but actually to ride it to the top (Kleiner, 2008).

To this day, Shell continues to develop scenarios for the future of global energy and make these publicly available on its website. The practice of scenario planning has also spread across the business world and other fields, including national security (National Intelligence Council, 2004; National Intelligence Council, 2008). This chapter describes how we used a similar scenario-planning process at McREL to think about the unthinkable and develop the four scenarios presented in this book.

Our Scenario-Planning Process

As the Royal Dutch Shell example illustrates, scenario planning is a process of envisioning possible futures to help anticipate and prepare for changes beyond our control. A scenario is not a prediction, nor is it complete fiction; rather, it is a *plausible* future reality based on data and careful analysis of trends—including both critical uncertainties and predetermined events.

Scenario planning is different from other kinds of planning. Instead of anticipating steps in a more or less straight line—projecting our future actions years in advance—it recognizes that, like the line from the famous Robert Burns poem "To a Mouse," the "best laid schemes of mice and men, go often askew." Thus, scenario planning explores uncertainties and how these uncertainties may interact with one another and predetermined events to upturn our best-laid plans.

Our Focal Issue

All scenario planning begins with a carefully crafted strategic question, or *focal issue*, which helps to limit the exploration of future trends. In our case, we focused on this question: "What will teaching and learning look like in 2020?"

At first blush, this question may appear rather straightforward, if not simplistic. But, in fact, it is stated in such a way as to focus our attention on several significant issues. Most notably, by focusing on "teaching and learning" rather than on, say, "American education" or the "educational system," we have not confined our view of the future to include the current system of education. We know that the current system may change, and, indeed, some of the scenarios we have written describe some of these potential changes.

Our Critical Uncertainties

Our methodology for developing these scenarios closely followed guidance from Peter Schwartz, former head of scenario planning at Royal Dutch Shell, who became the cofounder and chairman of Global Business Network. Based on his experience in scenario planning, Schwartz suggests distilling all of the trends that are likely to influence the future into just two *critical uncertainties* that relate to the focal issue (see, for example, Ogilvy & Schwartz, n.d.). The two critical uncertainties form the x and y axes of a Cartesian plane, with the resulting four quadrants of the graph representing four possible resolutions to these uncertainties, or scenarios of the future. This is the *scenario framework*. Certainly, more complicated scenarios could be built with the addition of other uncertainties, but the resulting complexity (a Cartesian space with three axes, for example, creates a cube of eight different scenarios) is often more confusing and nuanced than helpful.

We identified our critical uncertainties after exploring the broad range of factors from a wide array of areas—including economics, politics, demographics, technology, and contemporary culture—that we believed were likely to drive change in the future. This is not easy work. We struggled over the course of many meetings to identify the right critical uncertainties and how to label the ends of these axes, knowing that the rest of our scenario-building process would depend on the framework created in this step.

The two uncertainties we used to create our scenario framework were:

1   Outcomes of education (see fig. 1.1, critical uncertainty #1)

2   Direction of reform (see fig. 1.2, critical uncertainty #2, on page 17)

Critical Uncertainty #1: Outcomes of Education

This first critical uncertainty relates to the historic relationship between how we as a society define the desired outcomes, or measures of success, for the educational system and the students the system serves—whether through measuring student progress against a set of *standardized* outcomes or by allowing, indeed, even expecting, varied, or *differentiated*, outcomes for students, based upon their learning needs and life aspirations.

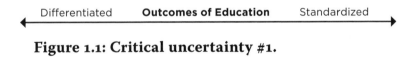

Differentiated   **Outcomes of Education**   Standardized

Figure 1.1: Critical uncertainty #1.

American education today seems to have planted its policies squarely in the ground of demanding a *standard* set of outcomes for all students. These outcomes might be described as: meeting or exceeding state-determined standards in reading, writing, and mathematics; graduating from high school; and being accepted into a postsecondary educational institution or finding a job that provides a living wage. Such a standard approach to defining outcomes ensures that policy does not allow different groups of students to be systematically undereducated or arbitrarily placed in "tracks" where expectations for academic success are lower and life choices fewer.

Moreover, the argument goes, with the dawn of the 21st century and its associated global, technological, economic, and other competitive challenges, who can afford *not* to be "college ready"? To demand anything less than 100-percent proficiency on high standards of knowledge and skill—from every single American student—would be foolish in a rapidly changing world such as ours. Not only is the standards movement strong, but a progression toward a common core of "fewer, clearer, higher" standards is moving rapidly across the nation to replace the hodgepodge of state standards currently in place.

At the same time, however, there is evidence of tension in the system, as some ask whether we might better meet the demands of a complex global economy by identifying, educating toward, and certifying the wide array of competencies required to meet its needs—be they academic, technical, or in some other category we have yet to imagine. As business writer Daniel H. Pink (2005) has argued in his bestselling book *A Whole New Mind*, it is our ability to be creative, to innovate, and to design new solutions to the dilemmas of a new age that will give America its competitive edge over the Asian countries, which are increasingly excelling in science and technology.

Proponents for a more differentiated approach to learning outcomes also ask whether graduation rates would improve and whether fewer children would be "left behind" if students were allowed to demonstrate variable competencies according to their own interests, aptitudes, and personal achievements. Certainly the customization of every other aspect of our lives, from the home page on our laptop computers to the ringtone of our cell phones, lends support for differentiating the outcomes of learning. Perhaps moving from a standardized approach to defining outcomes for learning on a student-by-student basis could be a win-win, differentiation advocates wonder—as long as issues of equity and fairness are addressed as we build (or rebuild) the system.

Critical Uncertainty #2: Direction of Reform

The second critical uncertainty relates to the controlling theory of action among educators, policymakers, and society in general regarding what it will take to reform the educational system—whether we can "optimize" the current system, tweaking, improving, and revamping it here and there as needed, or whether we must abandon our current system altogether, blowing it up and starting over, so to speak, by engaging in a wholesale reinvention that results in a new system of schooling with few, if any, vestiges of the current one.

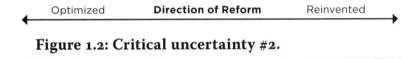

Figure 1.2: Critical uncertainty #2.

Since the publication of *A Nation at Risk* (National Commission on Excellence in Education, 1983), education reform has provided pundits, policymakers, and education professionals of every stripe with a mission: identify the *best* method for reforming the American educational system so that all students meet high standards of success. But what particular combination of curricular, pedagogical, and policy elements provides the best learning environment for ensuring that no child is left behind? It is safe to assume that over the next decade, attempts to reform education will continue. The uncertainty is whether the direction of those attempts will be toward sustaining the current system or toward building something new.

Sustaining, or optimizing, the educational system does not mean that nothing will change. Although system optimizers value the federal, state, and local structures that are in place to fund schools, to guarantee equity and quality of educational outcomes, and to provide accountability mechanisms appropriate for a public good, they also believe that more can be done to improve the system and its outcomes. The standards movement of the 1990s and the subsequent high-stakes accountability movement that began at the turn of the century are examples of efforts to optimize the current system. Indeed, NCLB, with its mandated state assessments, accountability provisions, and teacher-quality regulations, went further than any federal education law in history to grab hold of the existing components of the system and force them to work in the ways in which they were intended.

System reinventers, on the other hand, have set their sights on the "creative destruction" of the current system and construction of a new system as the key to success. These reformers have lost faith in all or parts of the current system and seek new, more outside-of-the-box strategies to meet the goals. Here is where we find proponents of vouchers, home schools, social networking and other cooperative learning environments, and many online learning providers.

In some cases, system reinvention is occurring unintentionally as a "disruptive innovation" in which individuals avail themselves of certain educational products, such as online courses, because they meet a specific need not being met by traditional schools. Over time, the innovation (for example, virtual schooling) becomes more satisfactory than the traditional system. The new world of learning may not be described as a system at all but rather the way in which education takes place.

In reality, the distinction between optimization and reinvention is subtle, and even a trend toward optimization of the current system, depending upon its nature, may in fact reinvent the system.

Our Scenario Framework

Graphing critical uncertainty #1 (outcomes of education) and critical uncertainty #2 (direction of reform) creates the scenario framework in figure 1.3 (page 20). Each of the four quadrants provides a basis for a scenario:

- "Test Day at Bronx City Day School" depicts the optimized/standardized quadrant, where educational outcomes have been standardized for all students and the current system has remained more or less intact, having been optimized, not reinvented.

✖ "Education to the Max" depicts the optimized/differentiated quadrant. In it, schools, districts, state agencies, and the other familiar trappings of the current educational system have survived in 2020. However, desired outcomes for students are now differentiated, taking into account each child's unique talents, interests, and aptitudes, as well as the business community's need for a diversified workforce with a wide range of skills.

✖ "Who Killed Buster the Bearcat?" depicts the reinvented/standardized quadrant, where educational technology—specifically, online schooling—and a long period of economic stagnation and prolonged school funding crises have resulted in traditional schools being replaced by online learning providers. Yet while the delivery of education has been reinvented, the outcomes have remained constant—rigidly fixed to a regimen of assessments that track students' progress against their national (and international) peers.

✖ "My Path to Juilliard" depicts the reinvented/differentiated quadrant, where social networking tools, the economy, and changes in consumer habits along with dissatisfaction with traditional K–12 education have resulted in a grassroots revamping of education, creating a technology-supported, "to each his own" system of education in which students are allowed to freely explore the world and learn according to their own interests and career aspirations.

For each scenario, a short abstract of its key features is followed by a summary of what we call the "deep causes" for the scenario. Deep causes answer these questions: What would have to happen between now and 2020 to cause the world described in this story to come about? What is the evidence that lays the foundation for the scenario? Specific information that adds to the plausibility of each quadrant's scenario is also provided. (Much of the evidence for the scenarios is described in chapter 2, including research on trends in the domains of economics,

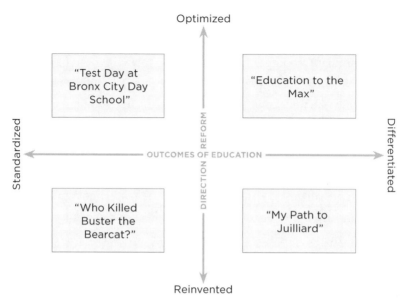

Figure 1.3: Scenario framework.

population, technology, and education policy.) Then, we present the scenario itself.

As you immerse yourself in the scenarios, you are likely to experience some discomfort with certain aspects of the worlds that are depicted. This is to be expected. The framework itself is challenging and, in some cases, shows education to be very different from what we know today. But ask yourself, Could these stories of the future become reality? Are they plausible? If so, are there actions that you could take today to get ready to survive and thrive within these worlds? Or are there actions you could take to nudge the future in the direction you prefer? With whom would you like to discuss these stories? How might you use them to spark conversations about your own organization's plans for the future?

Using the Scenarios

Scenarios are not intended to be simply thought experiments or mere academic flights of fancy; their purpose is to influence decision making, to guide action, and to shape strategic planning decisions. This section describes how you can use these scenarios to guide action in your districts, schools, and communities.

Interpreting the Scenarios

After the stories are written, the important work of interpretation begins. In other words, after delving into the "what if" questions that helped create the scenarios, we turn to the "so what" questions that inform strategic planning. At the end of each chapter, we offer questions that will prompt you, your colleagues, and your community to ask yourselves: If we were to find ourselves living in this world, what strengths would we have that would help us to survive and thrive? What would our weaknesses be? Are there opportunities for us here? Where are the threats? By going through this type of analysis, you will be able to see more clearly where the gaps may be in your preparedness for the future.

We also identify several *indicators*—events, trends, and other data— that we would expect to see if the scenarios are coming to fruition. Finally, each chapter will invite you to explore *options* that you might implement as part of a strategic plan in order to prepare yourself or your organization for the future. For this step, we recommend that you imagine that it is 2020 and that you are living in each scenario. We ask you to imagine that your students are succeeding beyond your wildest dreams on the full array of performance-based assessments that now constitute the accountability system. We recommend that you list all the activities you can imagine yourselves or your school districts undertaking to create that success. What is everyone in your organization doing to support this success? What have you done over the past decade to arrive here?

Determining Common Themes

The next step requires taking a look at the options for action that you develop for all four scenarios and determining any common themes.

Are there any actions that appear in all four quadrants? These could be *robust options*, which make sense to pursue *now* because they would pay off in any possible future. Options that look especially intriguing but appear in only one quadrant are called *bet-the-farm ideas.* They might look tempting, but it would be wise to carefully monitor the indicators to know if it makes sense to invest in them. After all, scenarios are not predictions! You don't want to "lose the farm" if a particular scenario does not turn into reality.

Asking "What If?"

Ultimately, perhaps the most important purpose of scenario planning is to force everyone within an organization or community to step outside of their current assumptions and mindsets in order to make better decisions. Just as managers at Royal Dutch Shell learned to evaluate their every decision against their company's scenarios, those in education can also benefit from constantly asking, "What if?" What if what lies ahead is radically different than what came before? Can we imagine that? Scenarios can help us envision a future no one has yet seen, and scenario planning can help us develop the strategies we need to prepare to meet its challenges.

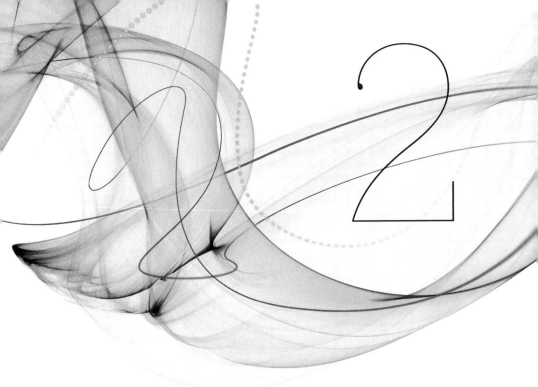

Drivers of a Changing World

Although much about the future is uncertain, there is information all around us today that helps us make sense of what is likely to occur tomorrow. Trends reveal patterns of behavior that help to resolve some of the uncertainty about the future. Things *will* change. But we can, as R. Buckminster Fuller charges us, become "architects of the future" rather than its victims—if we examine what we know about the world and consider the likely implications of that knowledge.

In this chapter, we summarize the key trends we believe have had and will continue in the coming decade to have a profound impact on the nature of American schooling. We do not offer this as an exhaustive review of our, or of others', research on this topic. Rather, we provide information in four domains—economy, technology, population, and education policy—in order to lay a foundation for the scenarios that follow and to stimulate thinking about the ways in which these forces may be influencing change.

Economy

The U.S. economy is incredibly resilient. Despite various panics, recessions, and one depression, when viewed from the long arc of history (a one-hundred- or two-hundred-year perspective), the American economy has continued on a steady upward trajectory of progress and prosperity. At the time of this writing, however, the U.S. economy is suffering from one of the worst downturns in several decades, and this is a factor in each of the scenarios discussed in this book. Nonetheless, given that the larger trend for the U.S. economy is steady growth, it is reasonable to assume that, at some point, the economy will recover.

As of this writing, current forecasts from the Congressional Budget Office (CBO) call for the economy to begin to recover, albeit slowly, in 2010, returning to 4 percent growth by 2011 and 2012 (Congress of the United States, 2009). However, some economists, including University of Maryland economist Peter Morici, worry that a double-dip recession could turn the coming decade into a repeat of the 1930s. In July 2010, Morici told the *Denver Post*, "If the economy goes down for a second time, then it likely goes down for good" (Svaldi, 2010). Brookings Institution Fellow Alice Rivlin (2009), former director of the CBO, cautioned during congressional testimony in January 2009, "Right now I think we should be skeptical of all forecasts and especially conscious of the risk that things may continue to go worse than expected" (p. 2). Nobel Prize–winning economist and *New York Times* columnist Paul Krugman (2009) has frequently written that "this isn't your father's recession—it's your grandfather's recession." Similarly, popular financial consultant Suze Orman (2008), in her book *Suze Orman's 2009 Action Plan: Keeping Your Money Safe and Sound*, writes, "My sense is that we could be in for a long, slow period of recovery and it will be 2014 or 2015 before the economy is back in robust good health" (p. 6).

Economists remain divided as to the "shape" the economic recovery is likely to follow—whether it will be the dreaded L-shape (falling sharply and taking several years to recover, akin to Japan's "lost decade"), V-shaped (rebounding quickly), U-shaped (rebounding more slowly), or W-shaped (going up and down before recovering) (Foroohar, 2009). By mid-2009, many economists had come to believe that the recovery would be W-shaped, rising in response to stimulus spending but then going back down as the dollars printed by central banks around the world to pay for stimulus packages lead to inflation, stalling recovery (Foroohar, 2009).

In September 2009, Federal Reserve Chairman Ben Bernanke declared that the recession had ended, while cautioning that it would take some time before unemployment rates dropped as well (Labaton, 2009). This announcement came along with significant cautions and an indication that the rate of the anticipated recovery would be moderate at best.

Some of our scenarios do, in fact, reflect the U.S. economy recovering. Yet we can envision three key events or trends delaying a recovery—or worse, leading to a deep and prolonged period of economic contraction:

1 Rising energy costs

2 Increasing costs of entitlement and health care

3 Federal deficits spurring inflation and/or a devaluation of the U.S. dollar

A long economic slump could have a tremendous impact on the future of schooling—especially if it is coupled with continued increases to government entitlement programs, such as Medicare and Social Security. Squeezed by declining tax revenues and increasing entitlement costs, lawmakers would likely face tremendous pressure to cut education funding, and educators would be forced to make dramatic cuts in spending. Indeed, a deep cause for two of our scenarios—those that reflect dramatic, technology-driven transformations in education—is a long period of economic stagnation or decline, which we envision would create considerable demand for cheaper, more efficient alternatives to traditional models of schooling.

Rising Energy Costs

As gasoline climbed to over $4 per gallon and oil peaked well over $100 per barrel in the summer of 2008, many pundits projected that the world's "oil peak"—that is, the point at which demand begins to outstrip production, leading to an inexorable rise in prices—was close at hand. Some projected the peak would occur as early as 2009, while others predicted the peak might occur in 2019 or later. Jeff Rubin (2009), former chief economist of the Canadian CIBC World Markets bank and author of the book *Why Your World Is About to Get a Whole Lot Smaller*, predicts that rising demand from China, India, and other emerging economies, coupled with limited supplies, is likely to cause the price of oil to skyrocket, setting off numerous ripple effects, including increased transportation costs that all but bring an end to international trade, reversing the trend toward globalization. In addition, food scarcities will become a number-one concern for many countries, especially those lacking arable land (Crooks, 2009).

However, several oil industry observers have argued that the case for peak oil has been overblown. Among them is Michael Lynch, an energy consultant and former director for Asian energy and security at the Center for International Studies at the Massachusetts Institute of Technology. Lynch wrote an op-ed in the *New York Times* that points to the discovery of huge new oil fields in the deep waters off the coasts of West Africa, East Africa, and Latin America as evidence that known supplies of oil in the world continue to increase at a rapid rate. In it, Lynch (2009) argues that "perhaps the most misleading claim of the peak-oil advocates is that the earth was endowed with only 2 trillion barrels of 'recoverable' oil." According to Lynch, "the consensus among geologists is that there are some 10 trillion barrels out there." As a result, he projects that any peak in production is likely decades away and that, in the short term, newfound reserves and technologies to exploit them would likely drive *down* the cost of oil to its "historic level of $30 a barrel."

Increasing Costs of Entitlement and Health Care

In May 2009, the trustees for Social Security and Medicare predicted that by 2016, Social Security will begin to spend more money than it takes in through tax receipts and that the trust fund would be depleted by 2037—four years earlier than previous projections. The trustees' assessment of Medicare solvency was more dire, predicting that the program designed to provide health care to elderly citizens would be depleted by 2017—two years earlier than previous projections (Goldstein, 2009). While some economists, such as Robert Reich, insist that fixing the potential insolvency of the Social Security system could be done relatively painlessly by raising the retirement age as well as the ceiling on annual income subjected to Social Security taxes, most agree that Medicare is a more serious concern (Froomkin, 2009).

Federal Deficits Spurring Inflation and/or a Devaluation of the U.S. Dollar

In October 2009, Moody's credit rating service warned that if the United States does not reduce its budget deficits significantly within the next three to four years, it is at risk of losing its AAA credit rating for the first time since 1917 (Reuters, 2009). David Walker (2009), former comptroller general of the United States and current president of the Peter G. Peterson Foundation, warned in a May 2009 *Financial Times* op-ed that "one of two developments could be enough to cause us to lose our top rating": (1) Congress passes health-care reform that increases, rather than reduces, "the huge unfunded healthcare promises" already made; and (2) Congress fails to show fiscal restraint "after we turn the corner on the economy," which would "send a signal [to foreign investors] that our political system is not up to the task of addressing the large, known and growing structural imbalances confronting us."

In his 2007 book *The Black Swan*, Nassim Nicholas Taleb describes how throughout history, "black swan events"—that is, circumstances that no one thought possible until they actually occurred (just as everyone believed swans to be white until black swans were discovered in Australia)—have consistently surprised experts and proven conventional wisdom wrong. Some examples of black swan events include the rise of Google, the attacks of 9/11, and a category 4 hurricane (Hurricane Katrina) reaching and overwhelming the levies of New Orleans. He claims, in fact, that almost all important historical events have come from the unexpected and notes that financial markets are particularly vulnerable to such events (Taleb, 2007).

In recent years, some economists and investors have cautioned that current actions to alleviate the economic crisis in the short term could have disastrous (that is, black swan–like) long-term consequences by ballooning deficits and driving up interest rates. In early 2009, Warren Buffett, concerned that high levels of government spending would lead to an "onslaught" of inflation, warned investors to stay out of treasury bills, as he predicted that government spending would devalue treasury bills and lead to a historic "bubble" in the value of treasuries (Stempel, 2009). Likewise, Alice Rivlin (2009) warned Congress in early 2009:

> We are lucky that, even though this world-wide financial crisis started in the United States, the response of world investors has been to flock to the safety of U.S. Treasuries, which makes it possible for our government to borrow short-term at astonishingly low rates. But we cannot count on these favorable borrowing conditions continuing forever. Especially if we fail to take serious steps to bring down future budget deficits, the United States government could lose the confidence of its foreign creditors and be forced to pay much higher interest rates to finance both public debt and private debt. Rapid increases in interest rates and a plummeting dollar could deepen the recession and slow recovery. (p. 3)

On February 22, 2005, reports that the central bank of South Korea was shifting reserves from U.S. dollars into sounder currencies caused the dollar and stock market to plunge—until the reports were eventually denied. Nonetheless, David M. Walker, then accountant in charge of the federal government's books, warned at the time that if federal deficits continued unchecked, it would be "inevitable" that the Asian banks financing U.S. federal deficits would lose confidence in the U.S. dollar and demand higher interest rates from the U.S. government. "The crunch is coming," Walker warned. "We are at risk. We are at serious risk" (Farrell, 2005).

In March 2009, Wen Jiabao, premier of China, the largest creditor to the United States (with $1 trillion in U.S. treasuries), expressed concerns about the safety of its U.S. bonds. "We have lent a huge amount of money to the U.S., so, of course, we are concerned about the safety of our assets. Frankly speaking, I do have some worries," said Wen during a press conference (Batson & Browne, 2009). While Wen asserted that his government would not act rashly or do anything to destabilize international markets, Wen's comments raised concerns that China may reduce or halt future purchases of U.S. debt. According to some analysts, China turning off its credit spigot would drive up U.S. interest rates, further pushing down home prices and, in a worst-case scenario, starting a run on the dollar (McCullagh, 2009). In its 2009 policy bulletin, the Cato Institute envisioned just such a scenario: a black swan event in which untamed deficit spending could lead to a "catastrophic collapse" scenario resulting from "a loss of investor confidence in the creditworthiness of the U.S. government" and creating a situation "many times worse than the Great Depression" in which "economic activity would decline by 90 percent or more" (Kling, 2009).

Technology

One trend that we can safely assume will continue to play out through 2020 and beyond is the exponential growth in technology. Moore's law, a concept defined by Intel cofounder Gordon Moore in 1965, states that the number of transistors on a chip doubles about every twenty-four months. In other words, if Moore's law continues to hold true, the technologies considered cutting edge in 2010 will only be half as fast or powerful as those that will emerge in 2012, which will themselves only be half as powerful as those in 2014, and so on.

Smaller, Cheaper, Faster

We can also assume that devices that connect to the Internet, such as netbooks and smartphones, will continue to become smaller and more ubiquitous. According to the U.S. Census Bureau, the number of cell phone subscribers in the United States rose from 34 million in 1995 to approximately 109 million in 2000, just five years later. In 2005, five more years later, there were nearly 208 million cell phones in use in the United States (U.S. Census Bureau, 2007). The latest estimate (2008) is that there are roughly 270 million cell phones in use in the United States (Central Intelligence Agency [CIA], 2008). With the U.S. population estimated at over 309 million (U.S. Census Bureau, n.d. *a*), this means that we are rapidly approaching and will likely exceed at least one cell phone for every human being living in the United States. What's more important is that most of these phones have far more features than simply making and receiving calls. Many are, in effect, small computers with more processing power than the computers on *Apollo 11* (Nelson, 2009). And we carry them in our pockets and purses!

In addition to faster processing speeds and more memory, we can also assume that the cost of technology will continue to decline. A case in point: one of the authors of this publication bought a laptop in 2002. The laptop cost over $3,000 and had 16 gigabytes of storage and 512 megabytes of RAM. The computer was considered top of the line at the time, yet it did not come with a wireless card or a built-in webcam or microphone. In July 2010, a laptop with *8 times* more RAM (4 GB) and *31.25 times* more storage (500 GB) retailed for about a quarter of the price of the 2002 laptop, just $700, and included a built-in wireless card, webcam, microphone, and full suite of software. With today's emerging netbooks, the $99 iPhone, and open-source software, technology is becoming more and more accessible to those who could not have previously afforded it. Instead of creating a "digital divide," it is entirely possible that technology could play a role in providing access to quality educational experiences to all, regardless of geographic location or income level.

Social Networking

More and more people are using technology not only to automate any task that can follow a protocol, including learning tasks, but also to create and participate in powerful and diverse communities. We are now a society accustomed to having access to information and colleagues 24/7—from any location—and to using social networking tools such as Facebook, Meetup, Twitter, and Ning to help us do so. How much longer can we reasonably expect students to sit in classrooms for eight hours a day, five days a week, following a regimented curriculum with relatively narrow outcomes, in light of this context, student interests, and their future careers?

Disruptive Innovations

In *Disrupting Class: How Disruptive Innovation Will Change the Way the World Learns*, Clayton Christensen, Michael Horn, and Curtis Johnson (2008) predict that, over the next ten years, online learning could dramatically alter how education is delivered. They project that 50 percent of all high school courses will be delivered online by 2019. The *disruptive innovation theory* they advance states that, in nearly every industry, companies are constantly improving their products. Generally speaking, though, these innovations are usually incremental or "sustaining"—they consist of making "airplanes that fly farther, computers that process faster, cellular phone batteries that last longer, and televisions with clearer images" (p. 46).

Every industry, however, has "nonconsumers"—people who are unable to consume the products or services that are provided. For example, in the 1970s, mainframe computers were too expensive for all but the largest companies to buy. Even so-called minicomputers cost upwards of $200,000 and, thus, were priced well out of the range of household consumers. However, starting in the late 1970s and early 1980s, Apple began building computers for these nonconsumers. The personal computer was originally designed as a toy for children, who didn't care if it wasn't as powerful as the mainframe and minicomputers their parents used at work. Over time, these "toy" computers became more powerful, faster, and graphic rich—and they fostered a whole new market of software and games to run on them. Eventually, in the late 1980s, the computer industry hit a tipping point, during which personal computers linked together on local access networks rapidly replaced mainframe computers, causing the demise of many once-proud mainframe computer companies.

The field of education, according to Christensen and his coauthors (2008), has remained fairly immune to disruptive innovation in part because traditionally there have been few nonconsumers—that is, students taught outside the system of traditional public schools. By law, most children are required to attend school. As a result, although education has adapted to the many changes society and federal legislation have required of it (consider, for example, desegregation and new forms of accountability), education has not undergone the same kinds of disruptive change other fields have experienced. Digital technologies have changed the face of many other industries—including retail, entertainment, and telecommunications—yet have had little impact in changing the way education is delivered. Schools continue to view teachers as the core technology of the learning process, even though, conceivably, computers might be used to provide more engaging and individualized instruction to students.

For the moment, though, instruction delivered via a computer is still inferior to what students can receive from a local, live teacher. However, for nonconsumers of education—the one million students now homeschooled or the 30 percent of students who drop out of traditional schools—computer-based learning *may* represent a real improvement (Christensen et al., 2008). While computer-based learning technologies remain outside of the mainstream (less than 1 percent of K–12 courses are currently delivered online), they are rapidly improving to serve the needs of this growing class of education nonconsumers (Christensen et al., 2008).

Christensen and his colleagues (2008) identify four factors that could accelerate the rate of learning-technology adoption: (1) ongoing improvements to computer-based learning, making the courses more engaging than traditional teaching; (2) the ability of students, teachers, and parents to adapt students' learning experiences to their interests and needs; (3) teacher shortages, especially in hard-to-staff areas and subjects; and (4) falling costs of computer-based learning coinciding with federal, state, and local budget crises caused by the unfunded liabilities for government retiree health-care costs (an estimated $600 billion to $1.3 trillion) bankrupting many state and local governments.

Open Education Resources

Coupled with online learning is an explosion of open-source, open-access curricula, including resources such as Curriki (www.curriki.org), CK–12 (www.ck12.org), MIT OpenCourseWare (http://ocw.mit.edu), and University of the People (www.uopeople.org).

Access to new curricula has the potential to have an impact far beyond K–12 students. Going back to traditional schooling every time one wishes to change jobs or update his or her skill set doesn't make sense anymore. Technology could result in a major shift in the traditional learn/work/leisure cycle that is developing from extended life spans and multiple careers within a lifetime. It is increasingly likely that we will turn to open-source, open-access means of educating ourselves.

It is difficult to imagine any future world in which technology does not play a starring role. Even though the United States may be in a long period of economic decline, technology appears to be on a relentless path toward ever greater power at ever less cost, thoroughly infusing itself into every aspect of our lives. Indeed, just as Shell scenario planners in the early 1970s viewed rising global demand for oil as an inescapable reality, we have viewed advancement in information technology over the coming decades as a predetermined event and therefore likely to appear in each of our scenarios. However, other forces that vary from quadrant to quadrant will affect the way in which technology is utilized in the various worlds we have envisioned. Technology is present and at times dominant in our scenarios, but nowhere is it seen as the *complete* solution to education reform.

Population

Because population data are consistently collected over long periods of time by the U.S. Census Bureau and by marketers, they can provide more certainty to a scenario. In fact, population is often considered one of the predetermined elements in a scenario. And yet, uncertainty is still inherent in population data in terms of the way in which we as a society respond to the opportunities and challenges presented by population changes.

The following sections describe specific aspects of the population with implications for education. "Race and Ethnicity" explores the proportional increase of minority populations in the United States and implications for schools as they are faced with changing student and family characteristics. "Aging" describes the challenges and opportunities presented to schools by a society that is becoming, on average, older. "Generations" examines the unique characteristics of different age groups and how these age groups act, and interact, in schools and society. The final section, "The Fourth Turning," describes the context in which all of these forces will play out in the next few years, a period of crisis and renewal.

Race and Ethnicity

The racial and ethnic composition of students and families is changing. The language and cultural backgrounds of students in a school, and even a classroom, will be increasingly varied and diverse. Indeed, according to the U.S. Census Bureau (2008), more than half of all children in the United States will be racial or ethnic minorities by 2023. This "majority minority" student population will primarily be composed of Hispanic students; nearly one in three United States residents is projected to be Hispanic in 2050. This is known; what is unknown is how schools will respond to these changes to meet the needs of all students.

Hispanics are the largest minority group in twenty-two states, and according to 2006 data, the vast majority—84 percent—of Hispanic public-school students were born in the United States (Fry & Gonzales, 2008). As education is tasked with meeting the needs of these diverse students, statistics regarding culture and language indicate potentially challenging circumstances for educators. For example, according to the U.S. Census Bureau (2008):

> More than one-in-four Hispanic students live in poverty, as do more than one-third of non-Hispanic black students. This is markedly greater than poverty rates for non-Hispanic white students (11 percent). Additionally, a significant number of Hispanic students have parents who have not completed high school (34 percent) compared with non-Hispanic students (7 percent). In addition, 70 percent of Hispanic students speak a language other than English at home.

Each of these characteristics presents challenges to education. Poverty is associated with lower measures of health, achievement, and behavior in children (Brooks-Gunn & Duncan, 1997), and lower levels of parental education are also associated with lower levels of academic achievement (National Center for Education Statistics, 2008). The same is true for students who are in the process of acquiring English language proficiency (National Center for Education Statistics, 2009). Taken together, these data paint a picture of the challenges and opportunities posed by the changing demographic picture in public schools in the imminent future.

While Hispanic students will be the majority of minority students in the school system, a broad spectrum of nonwhite students will also present unique needs. One need only look at the plurality of languages in which educational materials are being offered, particularly in urban systems; for example, the *Parent/Student Handbook of the Los Angeles Unified School District* (Los Angeles Unified School District, 2009) is available in English, Spanish, Korean, Armenian, Chinese, Russian, Farsi, and Vietnamese. The New York City Department of Education prints its *Family Guide* in nine languages, including Haitian Creole, Urdu, and Bengali (New York City Department of Education, 2009).

As the proportion of white students decreases relative to minority students, non-Hispanic white students will increasingly become less isolated from minority students while their minority student peers will become *more* isolated from them, at least while in school. In other words, in the public schools, minority students will become the majority, creating a subculture of racial and ethnic experience different from that of the rest of society. As proportionally fewer white students mix with greater proportions of minority students, the decades-old battle to desegregate the public schools in order to guarantee equity in the allocation of resources and to promote racial tolerance will need to continue. Indeed, not only will minority students become further segregated from their white peers, but data show that, even now, black and Hispanic students are isolated from *each other*, as majority-Hispanic schools have very few black students and vice versa. Though other factors influence the degree of segregation in schools (such as geographic dispersions of populations and school desegregation policies), the increasing proportion of minorities in the student population will present challenges to desegregation (Fry, 2007).

For English-language acquisition for new immigrants, for successful cross-cultural integration among students and school community members, and for the ability of individual schools to meet the pressing needs of low-income children of color, schools must consider the implications of these data as they plan for the future.

Aging

As a nation, we are getting older. The median age of the United States population in 1998 was 35 years, compared with 23 years in 1900 (*TIME*, 1998). The median age is projected to peak in 2035 at 39.1 years as the Baby Boom generation (born between 1943 and 1960) ages and dies (U.S. Census Bureau, n.d. *b*). Average life expectancy increased by 30 years from 1900 to 2000; Americans are projected to have an average life expectancy of 79.5 years in 2020 (U.S. Census Bureau, 2009).

An aging population has significant implications for society and for education. For example, we have long been hearing about the impending retirement of the Baby Boom generation. The sheer size of this population segment (approximately 80 million) threatens to overwhelm the Social Security system as we know it today. This is in part due to the system of payroll contributions of current workers funding the benefits of current retired workers: the large number of people in the Baby Boom generation who are approaching retirement versus the smaller relative size of the generation who will be working and paying into the Social Security system as Baby Boomers retire and draw from it.

According to the Social Security Board of Trustees, by 2034 there will be only 2.1 workers for every beneficiary, down from 3.4 workers per beneficiary in 2009 (Social Security Administration, 2009). With fewer workers to support the growing ranks of retirees, the Social Security system will begin paying out more benefits than it collects from payroll taxes sometime around the year 2016 (OASDI Trustees, 2009). Unless policymakers are willing to take politically unpopular steps to increase payroll taxes for existing workers, reduce benefits for retirees (including raising the retirement age), or employ some combination of the two strategies, by the year 2037 the Social Security system will essentially go broke, expending all of its reserves and requiring a significant influx of additional funds to stay solvent (OASDI Trustees, 2009). While some may quarrel over the specific dates when Social Security outflows will exceed inflows and the system will expend its reserves, few debate the need for making hard choices to ensure the long-term sustainability of Social Security and other federal entitlement programs, including Medicare and Medicaid.

These facts are essentially predetermined. The uncertainty lies in how society will respond to our aging populations' needs and how the aging populations themselves will approach aging.

The United States may continue to place a priority on social programs that support the aged. Choices may be made to prioritize spending for entitlement programs for the aging over other programs, like education. Health-care reform may also reprioritize spending.

As individuals, members of the aging populations may rewrite the traditional model of retirement, choosing to pursue long-postponed second careers rather than leisure retirement. Baby Boomers may not find traditional retirement appealing and may take advantage of their relative robust health to continue to work and volunteer. They may prefer more moderate or holistic approaches to health care over intrusive treatments. They may find themselves caring for children or grandchildren who are unable to be fully independent in a recovering economy and so maintain relatively higher spending levels. They may simply not be ready to slow down or step aside.

Some of the scenarios examine these uncertainties. Entitlement programs continue to weigh down the economy; revitalized post-career volunteers and part-time workers support a reinvented education system; tension between generational preferences for education moderates the magnitude of change. In these scenarios, and in the future, these uncertainties create opportunities for strategic response.

Generations

Demographers William Strauss and Neil Howe (1991) make the case that generational contemporaries—those born during periods in which they experience the same formative events—develop unique characteristics that define them as a distinct "generation." Understanding these generational characteristics lends insight into behaviors and interactions that shape the present and future. Four distinct generations described by Strauss and Howe (Baby Boomers, Generation X, the Millennials, and the Homeland generation) play major roles in the four scenarios and shape the stories and outcomes. The characteristics of each generation provide a lens through which we can make sense of changing behaviors and evolving trends:

* **Baby Boomers** (born between 1943 and 1960) have tended to position themselves as the moral and cultural arbiters of society—from political correctness on the left to the preaching of the moral majority on the right—expecting younger generations to fall in line with their commandments. Raised during a time of affluence and Dr. Spock–influenced permissiveness, the "me generation" is known for its sense of entitlement as well as ideology. As they came of age, they fomented the consciousness awakening of the 1960s, followed by the "culture wars" of the 1970s, 1980s, and 1990s when society struggled to find its equilibrium somewhere between restrictive homogeny and excessive indulgence. They have focused their energies on righting wrongs and deeply identify with who they are and what they achieve at work.

* **Generation X** (born between 1961 and 1981) was born during a time of rising divorce rates, latchkeys, and open classrooms. As a result, Gen Xers have grown into a hard-edged, pragmatic, skeptical, resourceful, and independent generation. They bring a sense of free agency to the workplace and tend to have weak party affiliations in politics, as they have less faith in institutions and more faith in themselves as individuals. They have participated in an unprecedented technological revolution and are comfortable with multiple media, and they count on their peers and themselves to get things done. As Generation X moves into midlife, they form a pragmatic bridge between the ideals of the Boomers and the team-oriented aspirations of younger generations. This generation is the workhorse of the coming age, bearing the burden of transition and crafting workable solutions to problems of crisis.

* **The Millennial generation**, also referred to as Generation Y (born between 1982 and 1998), came of age during a time when society was generally more attuned to the needs of children

(evidenced by new books on parenting and an emphasis on character education and community service in schools). Strauss and Howe predict that as they enter the workforce, they will be more conformist, optimistic, and community-oriented than their predecessors, as they have been growing up in schools focused on higher standards, character education, cooperative learning, uniforms, and community service. They are comfortable in both virtual and physical space. They appreciate, and expect, diversity. And they are hard to bully, having had their opinions and input validated their whole lives. The Millennials, who are now moving into young adulthood, display teamwork and collective optimism that provides hope for a bright future. They are expected to ride to the rescue behind hardened Gen X generals, executing strategy with brilliance and energy.

- **The Homeland generation**, also referred to as Generation Z (born between 1999 and the present), are being raised in a more protected, post-9/11 atmosphere. As a result, they are predicted to be altruistic and humanitarian and to care deeply about social justice issues.

During the time period of concern in our scenarios, these four generations have parts to play. The general descriptions of generational characteristics reveal themselves in specific ways relative to education in the four scenarios.

Baby Boomers can be expected to exert their influence through their focus on righting wrongs and imposing their values on society. Baby Boomer educators identify deeply with their mission and believe they have earned the right, through experience and age, to direct the course of education rather than being told what to do. They are less technologically adept than the younger generations, which will exacerbate the sense of a "generational divide." They bring dedication to their cause and a wealth of experience to the table.

Generation X will become the majority parent population as the scenarios play out. Pragmatic and independent, they expect to be involved in decision making and don't simply defer to authority. They would prefer to have more say about their children's education and want their children to have choices as well. They are willing to work within a prescriptive educational system as long as they feel there are sufficient choices and that every student gets an equal choice (and an equally high-quality outcome). This generation has little loyalty to institutions, however. If the system cannot deliver, they will abandon it for something better.

Millennials are team players who enjoy collaboration. They also lack the deep-seated distrust of government and authority of their elder generations, as they have generally been well cared for and have grown up in times of stability and prosperity. They are technological wizards and thrive on instant gratification and constant, uninterrupted connection to their external world. In a look at the politics of this rising youth generation, Neil Howe and Reena Nadler (2009), writing for the New America Foundation, describe today's K–12 students (the Millennials) as "neotraditionalist" optimists who trust the system to solve big problems. The Center for American Progress published a study in 2008 that found that Millennials are more accepting of government oversight: "Millennials mostly reject the conservative viewpoint that government is the problem, and that free markets always produce the best results for society" (Madland & Logan, 2008, p. 1). As they mature and develop their own social contract with the government, they are expected to look for public agencies to provide order, facilitate community, strengthen markets, and ensure equity. Government, in their view, solves more problems than it creates, and they are willing to allow it to do its job. Thus, if a set of national standards will simplify the system and make it more rational, that will make sense to Millennials—as long as no one is left out. Moreover, this generation has no desire to "throw the baby out with the bathwater" if it's not necessary. They will work hard to build on what works and, in this sense, may seek to optimize (rather than reinvent) the current educational system.

In the scenarios, the Homeland generation is the generation of young learners, expecting learning experiences that they can mold and shape to their preferences. This generation also demands to be part of a community, be it virtual or physical.

Generational roles are played out regularly in schools today. For example, the very issue of school choice may reflect the values of Generation X parents. They value independence from traditional institutions of schooling and are resourceful in creating schools that they feel best meet the needs of their children as individuals.

School policies and conflicts over them may also be reflective of generational differences. For example, school administrators (Baby Boomers) may ban cell phones in schools, while parents (Gen Xers) believe their children need them, and the students (Millennials) seamlessly incorporate the phones, like other technologies, into their lives. Granted, these are simplistic generalizations, both of complex issues and of complex individuals, but they are also illustrative of how generational characteristics shape interactions and influence the direction of change.

The "Fourth Turning"

All of the forces of change described in this chapter occur within a larger national, or even global, context. Strauss and Howe's 1997 book *The Fourth Turning: What the Cycles of History Tell Us About America's Next Rendezvous With History* calls these contexts "turnings" and investigates the historical and modern characteristics of certain periods of time. A key thesis of Strauss and Howe's book is that history repeats itself every eighty to one hundred years in a series of four fifteen- to twenty-five-year cycles, or "turnings":

- The "first turning" is a period of general upbeat optimism, bordering on euphoria, called a *high* (such as the Gilded Age after the Civil War or the "American high" after World War II).

* The "second turning" is a period of *awakening*, a time of spiritual questioning, when the excesses of the previous era are questioned (such as the "transcendental awakening" of the early 1800s, the Progressive Era of the last two decades of the 1800s, and the "consciousness revolution" that began with the civil rights movement, continued with countercultural movements in the 1960s and 1970s, and culminated in the rise of the moral majority and the values-driven "Reagan revolution" of the early 1980s).

* The "third turning" is an *unraveling* era of pessimism. The individual is elevated above the collective, and people feel civility is declining, social bonds are fraying, and government institutions are ineffective (such as the Mexican War and Missouri Compromise era preceding the Civil War, World War I and prohibition, and the most recent period of "culture wars," during which it appears that the nation has become increasingly fragmented, public discourse less civil, and popular culture increasingly debased).

* The "fourth turning" is a *crisis* period (such as the Revolutionary War, Civil War, and World War II) during which society is challenged in multiple ways to redefine its norms, abandon unworkable ways of the past, and adopt a new civic order for a new age. Like the other periods, the period of the fourth turning typically lasts fifteen to twenty-five years, during which society experiences a climax of economic, social, cultural, ecological, military, political, or technologic distress. It is a period of discontentment, leading to the eventual establishment of a new order.

Through an examination of recent history, we can see society passing through an era of *unraveling*, heading rapidly toward a fourth-turning crisis. Writing in *USA TODAY* shortly after the terrorist attacks of 9/11, Strauss and Howe (2001) speculated that the fourth turning might have begun already, catalyzed by the terrorist attacks that spawned a "mood shift" in the United States, drawing Americans together in a sense of national purpose, unity, and willingness to identify and create "grand solutions" to the nation's challenges. If this fourth-turning theory plays out, we can expect a period of unrest and distress lasting until 2015–2025.

It is during this period of unrest and distress that the four scenarios occur. Societal reactions, driven by the generational characteristics described previously and the fourth-turning crisis, will drive change. Scenario planning provides the mechanism through which the uncertain outcomes of this change may be examined, and an understanding of these forces provides theoretical plausibility to the scenarios.

Education Policy

Our scenarios are framed within the standards-based accountability movement, the dominant policy theme in American education since the report *A Nation at Risk* (National Commission on Excellence in Education, 1983) and continuing through the reauthorization of ESEA in 2002 as the NCLB Act. The period of focus for the scenarios (2009–2020) coincides with the beginning of a new presidential administration that is setting a somewhat different course in education. Nevertheless, education policy, as stated by U.S. Secretary of Education Arne Duncan in a set of "reform principles," leaves the fundamental concepts of the standards-based movement intact. Secretary Duncan has created four reform principles for the use of the Investing in Innovation (i3) funds allocated under section 14007 of the American Recovery and Reinvestment Act of 2009 (ARRA):

> (1) Improvements in teacher effectiveness and ensuring that all schools have effective teachers, (2) gathering information to improve student learning, teacher performance, and college and career readiness through enhanced data systems, (3) progress toward college- and career-ready standards and rigorous assessments, and (4) improving achievement in low-performing

schools through intensive support and effective interventions. (U.S. Department of Education, 2009d)

NCLB set a target that all students would demonstrate proficiency
on academic standards by 2014. In 2008, halfway to the deadline, the
law had not been reauthorized or altered, no relief in the proficiency
target was granted, and schools and states were beginning to prepare
for what could be devastating fallout from earlier decisions. Nearly half
of all states had adopted a graduated approach to reaching the goal of
100-percent proficiency by 2014, meaning that, in early years, they set
lower targets, intending to catch up in later years. By 2008, these states
were facing targets to increase student achievement annually by 10
percent and higher in the remaining years. Even states with consistent,
incremental proficiency targets were having a difficult time. By some
estimates, only one-fourth to one-third of states were expected to
reach 2014 proficiency goals, and those may well have been states with
lower, easier proficiency standards (Chudowsky & Chudowsky, 2008).

Additionally, while there is confusion about the accuracy of reported
dropout rates, the most commonly accepted statistic reveals that around
30 percent of students across the nation do not earn a high school
diploma (*Education Week*, 2009).

Against this backdrop of a long history of standards-based accountability but with no real improvement in student achievement, educators
face two critical issues at the start of the scenario time period. These
issues play out in different ways in the various scenarios: (1) a shifting
societal viewpoint about standards, instruction, and assessment; and
(2) the uncertain impact of funds from the American Recovery and
Reinvestment Act (American Recovery and Reinvestment Act of 2009
[ARRA]), reputed to be the major policy lever for reform and dramatic
improvement across the American public education system.

Standards, Instruction, and Assessment

The American standards movement in education has a long history
in state and federal policymaking. And yet, in our globally competitive

society, it has become harder and harder to reconcile the tension in a system in which each state adopts its own content standards and associated measures of them. The results on the National Assessment of Educational Progress (NAEP) compared with the results on individual state exams show such gross disparities as to call into serious question the quality of states' own systems (Olson, 2007). When comparing American students against their international peers, the differences are even more pronounced (Gonzales et al., 2009).

In August 2008, *New York Times* editors argued that because "states have made a mockery" of NCLB's accountability provisions by "using weak tests, setting passing scores low or rewriting tests from year to year," it is impossible to compare progress, and therefore:

> Congress needs to take the testing issue head on. It should instruct the NAEP board, an independent body created by the government, to create a rigorous test that would be given free to states that agreed to use NAEP scoring standards. Then the federal government could actually embarrass the laggard states by naming the ones that cling to weak tests. Without rigorous and consistent testing, there is no way to know whether our children are getting the education they deserve and need. (Editorial Board, 2008)

Similarly, in April 2009, writers such as Walter Isaacson, former managing editor of *TIME* magazine and president and CEO of the Aspen Institute, began calling for *national* content standards, on the grounds that "clear standards, testing, and assessments would permit more experimentation by schools and individual teachers" and "parents and administrators can know which schools are successful" (Isaacson, 2009). Moreover, a *national* system of standards would allow for good ideas and successful innovations to be identified and transferred to new locations. As Isaacson (2009) put it:

> Indeed, the entire national debate about whether charter schools are good or bad could be defused (as Duncan did in Chicago) if both sides accept the obvious:

> good charter schools are good, bad charter schools are bad, and a system of common standards and assessment is needed to separate the wheat from the chaff.

Thus, the initiative launched in 2009 by the National Governors' Association (NGA) and the Council of Chief State School Officers (CCSSO) to develop a set of national standards in reading, writing, and mathematics that states would voluntarily adopt gained traction. (See the Common Core State Standards Initiative website at www .corestandards.org for more information.) The national test called for by the *New York Times* editors (Editorial Board, 2008) may also be just around the corner. The ARRA fund available to Secretary of Education Duncan includes $350 million for the development of just such a national assessment. At this writing, speculation abounds regarding what the Department of Education will request of the contractor or contractors competing for this funding, and the type of test that is hypothesized to emerge from the effort varies in our scenarios.

The push for *all* students to achieve a common set of "fewer, clearer, higher" standards (U.S. Department of Education, 2009b, p. 4) is rooted in a simple idea that has been evident since the inception of the standards movement. Essentially the premise is this: in light of past failures to educate all children well and the fact that many were left prepared for neither college nor the workplace, we must set high expectations for *every* student. Indeed, for many, the fight for equity in education equates with ensuring that *all* students be prepared for college, meaning they complete a rigorous college-prep curriculum with advanced placement courses and take college entrance examinations, such as the SAT and ACT. In short, for many, the standardization of desired outcomes for all students has been a civil rights issue—the continuation of a struggle that began with the *Brown v. Board* decision to ensure equal education for all students.

The "solution" of standardizing outcomes for students has not been without its detractors. Since the beginning of the standards movement, there have been concerns about meeting the needs of *individual* students whose own talents, interests, and inclinations might direct them down a path different from the college-prep/advanced-placement/SAT path. This desire for a student-by-student approach to learning is evidenced by the trend toward "portfolio schools" in districts such as Mapleton Public Schools in Colorado, where a variety of different schools designed to meet the needs of students with different learning needs and preferences have been established within a single school district. Another example of this individualized approach to learning is Big Picture Learning, which has established more than sixty schools in fourteen states that "embody the fundamental philosophy of Big Picture Learning, educating one student at a time in a community" (Big Picture Learning, n.d.).

The growth of charter schools and other public schools of choice, which developed at much the same time as the regular system of public education became increasingly standardized, appears to reflect a growing desire among parents and other consumers of public education for differentiated outcomes and pathways for learning. Public schools of choice that cater to individual learning styles (expeditionary learning, for example) or curricular focus (such as the arts or science and technology) have proliferated during the past decade, as have career and technical education (CTE) programs and school–business partnerships. The implicit belief underlying this proliferation and, indeed, underlying the school-choice movement in general is that each student has individual learning strengths and needs. It is a small step to further conclude that students will achieve educational success (that is, outcomes) in individual ways. In fact, several states have already begun offering paths toward differentiated diplomas, enabling students to receive technical diplomas or college preparatory diplomas (Education Commission of the States, 2008a, 2008b). In addition, a report by MDRC (Kemple & Willner, 2008) identified the positive benefits on earnings and life outcomes of programs that combine academic curricula with career and technical training. The authors claim that there are 2,500 of these programs, which they label "career academies," nationwide.

American Recovery and Reinvestment Act

The American Recovery and Reinvestment Act (ARRA) (American Recovery and Reinvestment Act of 2009), passed in the early days of the Obama administration, provided $100 billion for education. Both President Obama and Secretary of Education Duncan indicated these funds were to be used not only to save or create jobs, but to advance reforms and "get America on track to return to being number one in the world in high school and college graduation rates, school readiness, academic achievement, college matriculation and retention, and completion rates" (U.S. Department of Education, 2009b). The vast majority of the funds were distributed to states and local school districts by formula to enhance Title I and IDEA programs.

The best indication of the administration's priorities is revealed in its stated "assurances" for use of stimulus funding, including:

> college- and career-ready standards and high-quality, valid and reliable assessments for all students; development and use of pre-K through post-secondary and career data systems; increasing teacher effectiveness and ensuring an equitable distribution of qualified teachers; and turning around the lowest-performing schools. (U.S. Department of Education, 2009a)

The administration has also voiced support for charter schools, for alternatively prepared teachers, and for associating teacher and principal pay with student achievement (U.S. Department of Education, 2009c). From a political perspective, this represents a shift in that linking teacher and principal pay with student achievement has generally been associated with Republican administrations. We may postulate that trends in education are less dependent upon politics and more dependent upon other, perhaps more pragmatic, factors—including an overall weariness with the status quo and with reform agendas in general. So many things have been tried, so many resources have been expended, and still the needle of achievement hasn't moved enough to declare victory or even for us to feel that the nation is headed in the right direction.

In this environment, the notion of "reinvention" has appeared on the scene. Reinvention is part of the rhetoric of the education policy establishment of 2009. Some characterize a change from the hodge-podge of fifty unique state standards and assessments to a single set of national standards and one common assessment as a reinvention of the system. Others view such a change as merely a new form that is part of the same old system. Still others see reinvention as doing away with traditional notions of school buildings and classrooms in which students are grouped by age and taught by one teacher. Perhaps in the future there will be no more LEAs or SEAs (local education agencies or state education agencies) but rather networks of homeschoolers or individuals taught by "learning agents" who work as independent contractors and are known for their content and pedagogical expertise rather than the grade level they teach. Perhaps learning will take place online rather than in a face-to-face environment.

The extent to which ARRA funds may stimulate change in American schooling is a great uncertainty. The use and impact of the ARRA funds play out differently in the various scenarios.

Final Thoughts: A Metaphor for Planning in Uncertain Times

An outdoor wedding can be a beautiful occasion—music blends with birdsong, the bride looks radiant in the sun as she glides down an aisle of green grass toward the groom and bridal party. Outdoor ceremonies, however, can also be a wedding planner's worst nightmare. The most thoughtful, meticulous selections of dresses, caterers, music, and decorations can all be upturned by a sudden cloudburst, oppressive heat, or gusty winds, which can turn the ceremony into a catastrophe.

In the parlance we've used in this chapter, when it comes to wedding planning, several aspects tend to be more or less predetermined, such as the date, the location, the guest list, and, of course, the couple to be married. Looming over the event (especially an outdoor ceremony or reception) is a large critical uncertainty: the weather. What adds to the uncertainty is how people will respond to unexpected turns in the weather—with good humor (singing in the rain, perhaps), panic (fleeing to nearby vehicles), or morose resignation (calling off the wedding because it just wasn't meant to be). Prudent couples, of course, arrange backup plans in the event of inclement weather, such as reserving a nearby park shelter.

Educators, however, may not be so thoughtful when it comes to planning for their own organizations—where *many* critical uncertainties, not a single one like the weather, can come into play. It's easier, of course, to concern ourselves with the things we believe we can control—decisions like the selection of curricula, school sites, and staff development programs. Yet as we have illustrated in this chapter, many predetermined factors outside our control, such as demographic changes or technology innovations, are likely to change the face of education in the future.

At the same time, how we, as a society, respond to shifting demographics or to what uses we decide to put new technologies (for example, do we use technology to test kids more frequently or to allow them to pursue different, individualized curricular pathways?) will likely also alter the future of schools. Lastly, it's really anyone's guess how we will resolve competing impulses about education (for example, whether it's best to standardize or individualize learning outcomes for students).

Taken together, these predetermined trends and critical uncertainties make traditional approaches to planning, such as using current enrollment growth rates to project district enrollment rates into the future and plan capital construction projects accordingly, seem shortsighted—akin to meticulously selecting dresses, caterers, decorations, and music for an outdoor wedding without making contingency plans for unexpected turns in the weather.

The following chapters provide four very different visions of how these predetermined trends and uncertainties may interact with one another in the coming years to create future realities for educators and the students they serve. As noted earlier, our purpose in providing these scenarios is not to say these are the *only* four possible futures for education. Rather, they are designed to provoke your thinking about how different the future may be from what we know (and expect) today.

A question we've often asked ourselves in writing these scenarios is, What would need to happen for *nothing to happen* at all—that is, for education in the year 2020 to look exactly like it does today? Given the changes swirling all around us, like dark clouds brewing on the day of an outdoor wedding, if there's any outcome that seems the *least* likely, it's that nothing eventful will occur and that ten years from now, our schools will be mirror images of the ones we have today.

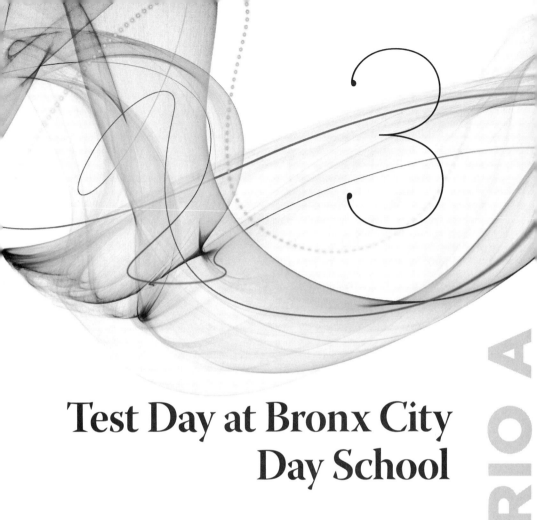

Test Day at Bronx City Day School

This scenario depicts a future in which the outcomes of education have been standardized for all students and in which the public values the current educational system, seeking to optimize, not reinvent, the system. This scenario takes into account a combination of policy initiatives beginning with the federal stimulus package (ARRA), which is used to shore up the framework of existing schools and districts in deep distress due to a failing economy instead of pushing for the abandonment of the current system in favor of something altogether new. In this scenario, we envision that ESEA is reauthorized with a focus on standardized outcomes and enhanced use of data to chart individual student performance. It's important to note that we envision school districts not as standing still, resolutely refusing to change, but rather engaging in ongoing improvements and adapting to external pressures—for example, co-opting the charter school movement through magnet schools and so-called zones of autonomy, empowerment, and innovation.

In this scenario, a group of Teach for America alumni is now into the sixth year of running a district-supported "empowerment school." They have built their school around the principles of a high-reliability organization (HRO) in which failure is not an option (Weick & Sutcliffe, 2001). Data are ubiquitous and utilized by teachers to make on-the-fly adjustments to instruction and to intervene at the first sign of distress in a student's academic life. Staff members work tirelessly to diagnose and refine their practices, resulting in an optimization of their performance. Although not every child is as successful as desired, most are continuously improving, and teachers are determined to see that, eventually, all students meet their goals.

Deep Causes

The writing of every scenario in this book began with a simple question: what key trends, or deep causes, would lead us toward this quadrant on our matrix? In the case of this scenario, which lies in the standardized/optimized quadrant of our matrix, we envisioned that such a future could come about as the culmination of several trends already evident in education today, including the push for national standards, federal support for developing better education data systems, an ongoing press to professionalize teaching through better pay and accountability, and generational transitions that lead to a society's more favorable disposition toward a "mend it, don't end it" approach to public education. The following sections describe these deep causes in more detail.

Standards and Assessments

In this scenario, today's increasing calls for national standards have been fully realized—born, in part, out of a reaction to today's disparate array of state standards and federal accountability measures spawning a "race to the bottom" among states seeking to avoid the long arm of federal sanctions. As the National Assessment of Educational Progress (NAEP) results reveal the discrepancies between scores on state assessments and its own rankings, we envision in this scenario that old arguments about local control have been drowned out with calls for "fewer, clearer, higher" standards (Isaacson, 2009).

The scenario is written just as the Council of Chief State School Officers (CCSSO) and the National Governors' Association (NGA) issue their call for states to join forces in the development of a Common Core of standards. The story assumes that this Common Core is established, along with a state-of-the-art assessment that can measure the identified knowledge and skills and can provide meaningful feedback to teachers and students. The assessment is a critical feature of the optimized system and dramatically improves the attractiveness of the Common Core to states. With a clearly defined set of standards and a test that reliably measures the knowledge and skills embedded in them, states can feel confident that "teaching to the test" will lead to improved student achievement.

An additional and perhaps stronger incentive to states to adopt the new national Common Core is the federal government's willingness, through ARRA and the subsequent reauthorized ESEA, to foot the bill. This is foreshadowed in Secretary of Education Duncan's progress report on his first one hundred days in his description of the Race to the Top (RTTT) Fund within the ARRA (Race to the Top Fund, 2009). He says the funds "lay the groundwork for dramatic, sustained progress in student achievement by supporting a vanguard of states who will adopt 'fewer, clearer, higher' standards and aligned assessments and data systems, all targeted to ensure college and career readiness" (U.S. Department of Education, 2009b, p. 4). States have been faced with enormous economic pressures from a combination of external global fiscal crises, along with internal factors in their own school systems, including unsustainable employee pension systems, crumbling infrastructure, and intolerable operating costs due to the rising price of energy. The cost of constantly updating state standards in many different subjects, as well as developing and scoring associated assessments, has become astronomical. District leaders are eager to direct their resources to other endeavors from which they hope to see more impact on student learning than the high-stakes accountability movement has so far produced.

Finally, in the guidance for grants under the secretary of education's discretionary RTTT program, states are expected to demonstrate that they have joined the effort to develop and adopt a "common set of K–12 standards that are internationally benchmarked and that build toward college and career readiness" (U.S. Department of Education, 2009c, Proposed Selection Criteria, [A] [A] [1] [i]). Although the current Common Core effort led by CCSSO and NGA is not named in the guidance, the implication is that states should affiliate with the project. Moreover, there is an expectation that states will join the effort to create an associated common assessment of the standards.

Use of ARRA Stimulus Funds

The RTTT Fund and the Investing in Innovation (i3) fund dollars, meant specifically to spur innovative reforms to the entire system, result in *improvements* but little or no real disruptive innovation to the system in this scenario. We hypothesize that this could occur due in part to the dire economic conditions facing states when the money is received, causing many to simply fill gaps or continue programs that are not succeeding. It could also occur if the funds support programs and approaches that aren't altogether different from current approaches and programs—for example, swapping old state standards for new national ones that in reality aren't much different from what was already in place, resulting in much sound and fury from state and local control advocates but signifying little to no substantive change.

This scenario imagines that by the year 2020, "empowerment" and "innovation" zones have popped up in many locations, creating district-sanctioned, charter-type schools, where employment waivers, used liberally in charter schools, pave the way for a transition in the teaching profession from the days of rewarding teachers for longevity to a system of pay based on their impacts on student achievement.

In this scenario, rather than reinvent the system, the stimulus funds are used to reinforce the existing system with a focus on superior execution. Tight controls for monitoring how states use the dollars are developed and implemented, and with one set of common standards and one national assessment, accountability is more easily achieved. The focus shifts to holding steady on the outcomes and increasing flexibility on how schools achieve them. Stimulus funds are used to create new data systems that improve the monitoring and reporting of system results, helping all the parts of the system to be more responsive to potential failures.

The Reauthorization of the Elementary and Secondary Education Act and the National Charter Schools Act

In this scenario, we envision that ESEA is finally reauthorized in 2012 as the All Children Exceed Standards (ACES) Act—a law that, among other provisions, requires states to adopt the Common Core and administer and report results of a newly created "Common Assessment," which is paid for by the federal government. In short, outcomes of a good American education will have been made clear by Congress.

Teacher Quality

The standardized/optimized quadrant represents a future world that places a high premium on the value of the teacher in the classroom as a lever for student improvement. Teacher recruitment, training, and retention are key targets of system optimizers. In 2009, Secretary of Education Duncan identified "increasing teacher effectiveness" among his expectations for use of the federal education stimulus funds. But he also made it clear that he does not equate traditionally trained and certified teachers with effectiveness: "Isn't all that matters that our children learn? That teachers give students knowledge? And not how they became a teacher, whether it's from a traditional route or an alternative certification route. At the end of the day, it is not about a piece of paper coming through the door. It's about student achievement" (Stengel, 2009).

This scenario extrapolates from the secretary's statement a world where today's largely input-based system of teacher certification and salary schedules (graduation from an accredited program, passing a PRAXIS examination, compensation based on years of experience and graduate degrees) has been replaced by an output-based system for determining teachers' fitness for the classroom and compensation (largely basing teacher hiring, firing, and compensation decisions on the academic performance of their students).

Certainly, in the past, many teachers' unions have resisted these measures. In this scenario, we hypothesize that unions' diminished resistance to linking performance measures to student achievement and merit pay could come about as the result of their own diminished political power or the unions' rethinking their positions on these issues, perhaps as the result of new generations of teachers emerging among the ranks of union leadership.

Policy, Politics, and Generations

Over the past several decades, education policy has consistently demanded higher standards and greater accountability for student achievement at the state and federal levels. This trend continues in this scenario. We envision that the generational characteristics of young Millennial professionals are influential in shaping an education policy environment supportive of optimizing, not reinventing, schools. Already in schools across America, we have seen young teachers, such as David Levin and Michael Feinberg, founders of the Knowledge Is Power Program (KIPP) schools, become social entrepreneurs, creating their own schools in response to the low achievement they have witnessed in the poor urban and rural school communities. We also see young

Teach for America corps members fresh out of college bringing youthful idealism to their positions, displaying a willingness to work long hours, and welcoming the framework of national standards, a common assessment, and the supports that come with the existing government framework of schooling. In this scenario, we imagine that these young teachers, who bring to their schools a unique mix of idealism (believing change is possible) and pragmatism (doing whatever it takes to make change happen), will mature into school leaders who are able to optimize the current system of education. They will do this, in part, by avoiding the rifts (such as reading and math wars, debates about school choice, and fights over constructivist teaching methods versus direct instruction) that divided previous generations and seemingly left education reformers lurching back and forth from one ideologically based reform to the next—rather than moving forward in a positive, optimizing direction.

Economy, Society, and Culture

The fourth turning is apparent in this scenario, but there are also signs of movement into the recovery period, with Millennials taking the lead on turning schools around. This scenario envisions that for much of the current decade, the economy has remained mired in a long recession, creating the conditions for states to accept the national Common Core of standards and the associated federally funded assessment—even if it means a loss of some local control. The scenario imagines that not all is perfect in this alternative future—for example, overcrowding and safety concerns still plague urban communities and schools. However, through a relentless focus on using data to continually optimize the system and hiring a new generation of teachers who are compensated for their hard work—and unceremoniously shown the door when their efforts fail to produce results—student achievement nationwide has begun to show steady gains by the time this scenario takes place, in the year 2020. Like a high-pressure valve cranked open just enough to let off a bit of steam, these steady gains in national student achievement, while maybe not breathtaking, have nonetheless reduced political pressure to seek radical new alternatives to the current system of public education.

The Scenario

Jasmine Diaz pulled her scooter into its usual spot under one of the few maple trees in the teachers' parking lot at the Bronx City Day School. As she slid her tiny frame off the bike and adjusted her backpack, making sure that the tofu and rice she packed for lunch hadn't spilled all over her laptop or her Kindle on the ride in, she took a deep breath and tried to put on her game face. "Today's the big day: test day," she thought, feeling a knot in her stomach from a mix of excitement and anxiety, not unlike how she remembered feeling when she was in high school herself and her volleyball team went to the state championships. Her students were prepared; she had no doubt about that. Her case of nerves, she told herself, was just from wanting them to do their best so they could show the rest of the city and state what great things were going on at Bronx City Day School.

Climbing the steps to the school (an old warehouse now converted), she smiled to herself and remembered, back in 2012, when she and a few other headstrong, idealistic Teach for America (TFA) alumni decided to take advantage of the closure of a middle school near the Bronx Zoo to petition the district to create their own "empowerment school." Jasmine and her colleagues were certain that they could create an environment for learning that would not only surpass anything they had seen during their two- or three-year stints as TFA corps members, but actually provide public school students with the same education opportunities as selective private schools. Thus, they arrived at the high-brow moniker, Bronx City Day School, an urban derivation of the "country day school" label for private schools found in leafy suburbs and urban fringes across the U.S. For two years, the district rejected their applications for a lack of clarity about what would actually help their students succeed where others had not. Jasmine and the school's current principal, Rita Cheevers, cornered a district official after a leadership meeting and convinced him that their school would use data in new and powerful ways, constantly improving instruction based on student progress while providing targeted learning supports that would help every student succeed, and their application was finally accepted. In 2014, Bronx City Day School was born.

A full six years later, in 2020, the school was still going strong, with 552 students in grades 6 through 12, serving the neighborhood in which it resided as an empowerment school. It had been a difficult six years, but they began their school committed to learning from mistakes, and they had managed to maintain that commitment—even when falling into a routine seemed so very appealing when things got tough and they all got tired. Though it had taken six years, they had reached a point where every teacher had the information and data necessary to make on-the-fly adjustments to teaching. There was no such thing as "rote teaching" in this school, and it was working; the kids were showing continuous improvement.

But Jasmine always worried on test day because, even though most students showed growth from year to year, not all were achieving at a rate that would ensure that they could go to college or get a high-paying job after high school—yet. Jasmine and her boss and friend, Rita, would not be satisfied until *all* students were succeeding.

Jasmine walked into the teachers' lounge and put her lunch in the fridge.

"Hey," said Dulcie, the seventh-grade teacher, looking up from a stack of papers she was grading. "Well, are we ready for this?"

Jasmine shrugged. "Ready as we'll ever be. I heard they made some changes to the test again this year. I hope it doesn't throw our kids for a loop. We've been on quite a roll lately."

"Four years and counting," Dulcie replied, referring to the school's steady streak of annual gains on the national assessment. "At least the computerized assessments keep their attention. I remember when I first started teaching, we had those stupid little bubble sheets. Sometimes the kids would space out or get frustrated and just start marking in Christmas trees."

"Or get off by a line and wind up missing half of the items in a section," Jasmine said, remembering the scene during her first year of teaching when one of her brightest students had come into her classroom in tears after learning that her anomalous low score on her state math test had prevented her from being placed into an advanced mathematics class.

Dulcie nodded. "That happened to a couple of my kids, too," she replied. "The worst part, though, was waiting until the next school year to get the results back. It was like trying to drive a car by looking through the rearview mirror."

Jasmine laughed. "I remember we nearly had a revolt once during a data-driven decision-making in-service session. The poor lady the district sent down to deliver the workshop nearly got tarred and feathered and run out of the high school auditorium on a rail. I remember my department chair asking her, 'How are we supposed to make data-driven decisions about *this* year's kids with data from *last* year's kids?'"

Dulcie smiled. "I would gladly endure a *month* of test days like we have them now before I'd go back to that. Now we only have to sweat it out for seven days, not seven months."

"I have to admit that when I first heard about all of the money that Obama and everybody else was plowing into data systems, I was pretty peeved," Jasmine said, as she poured herself a cup of coffee and dropped a couple of quarters into the community coffee fund. "I remember teachers were getting laid off, and I kept thinking, 'Seriously? Of all things we could be spending money on, we're going to waste it on this?'"

"I felt the same way," Dulcie agreed.

"But then I looked around and realized that we were laying off some really good teachers and keeping some really rotten ones," Jasmine continued as she clasped her hands around her coffee mug to warm them. "I remember asking my principal at the time, 'Why can't we be smart about this? We all know who the good teachers are and which ones are . . . well, just biding their time until they can collect retirement.' You know what he told me?"

Dulcie shook her head.

"He said, 'I would be making my cuts totally different if I could—and probably saving jobs while doing it, since I'd let go of some people who are up there on the pay scale. But I'm not *allowed* to make termination decisions based on student performance.' The next day, my best friend, who was an excellent teacher, got laid off," Jasmine said, pausing a moment to take a sip of coffee. "A charter school snatched her up in a heartbeat; she's still there. From that point on, I was like, 'Bring on the data.'"

"I'm right there with you," Dulcie said. "I once got in a big fight with my school's union rep about this. I kept saying, 'Look, I want the *world* to know how good a teacher I am.' She got steamed and just kept saying that I wasn't seeing the big picture. I said *she* was the one who wasn't seeing the big picture. A bunch of the younger teachers and I voted her out the next year, and she put in for a transfer to a different school. I sort of hated to see her go. She was a nice lady and did a decent job with her kids. Just kind of a dinosaur, though."

"Who's a dinosaur?" asked a man's voice. It was Roger, the reading specialist. He had walked into the lounge to put his lunch in the community refrigerator.

"Nobody," Jasmine replied, trying to change the subject as she knew Roger's political leanings.

"The union rep at my old school," Dulcie replied, not picking up on Jasmine's cue. "A total old-school, blue-collar, storm-the-Bastille type. If it were up to her, we'd still be using dartboards and dice to make teacher placements."

Jasmine winced. She knew what was coming.

"So you like this better?" Roger asked, his face growing red. "Giving kids ulcers so we can convince ourselves that we're teaching them? Using a biased, bogus test cooked up by someone in DC or Princeton or wherever they write these things, so that we can pin a number on a teenager, making or breaking his life, even before he's had a chance to learn *anything* about life?"

"Let's change the subject, guys," Jasmine suggested.

"I think you're exaggerating, Roger," Dulcie said. "It's not like that at all. The tests aren't *that* bad. And at least now we know if what we're doing is working."

"I can assure you that what we're doing is *not* working," Roger snapped. Jasmine braced herself. She could tell from the way he had straightened his back that he was about to get preachy. "Tell me, after these kids leave school, when will their merit be judged based on how well they can answer questions on a computer? We've created a whole generation of kids who are lost when they get to the real world, where they actually have to *think* for themselves."

"They were lost before, Roger," Dulcie replied, not backing down. "A third of our kids were dropping out. Another third weren't ready for college or the workplace. Now at least they have a fighting chance."

Dulcie had a point, Jasmine thought. She had just seen a headline reporting that fewer kids, only about 15 percent, were now dropping out of school.

Roger looked at Jasmine and Dulcie and shook his graying head. "I'm not angry with you two," he said, softening his tone. "I . . . well, I guess I am just a dinosaur, as you say. But I'm proud of it. Look, the union fought for protections that someday you'll wish you had. Like when your principal decides to give you a pink slip because she can replace you with someone who makes less money or because you spoke up and contradicted her in a faculty meeting. Or the district decides to lay you off two years before you're eligible for pension. Or someone in the central office decides to give your job to his cousin. We've lost all that protection. And we've also lost what education is all about: developing minds. Now all we care about is who can get the high score on our little video games," he added, referring to the computerized adaptive testing program the kids would be using shortly.

That prompted Jasmine to look up at the clock. It read 8:25. "T minus five minutes, guys. We'd better get going," she said, happy to bring an end to the tense conversation.

As Jasmine walked the halls to her classroom, she thought about Roger and whether it was a mistake for the school's principal to keep him around. He was a good teacher, but Jasmine grew weary of his negativity and yearning for the "good old days," which in her estimation weren't so good at all. When she and her TFA cofounders designed the empowerment school, they decided that it would adopt the characteristics of a high-reliability organization (HRO). They had read about HROs in organizational theory and saw the potential for applying the characteristics of an HRO to schooling—creating a school that relied on the constant use of data, where no failure was acceptable and where constant attention to improvement and reliable performance was ingrained. Jasmine and the others believed this was the perfect way to address the shortcomings of an educational system that viewed some kids as "acceptable losses," a system in which success often depended on whether or not your teacher cared enough to work hard. In their school, teachers were preoccupied with failure. They tackled hard problems and dug deep to solve them, and they learned from their mistakes, responding with improvements.

To have Roger constantly questioning the very source of the data they used to guide the school—the results of the national assessment and the benchmark assessments that led up to the annual test—was tiresome to say the least. Ironically, those very data that Roger challenged preserved his position at the school. Student reading results in the school were consistently among the best in the district, and the students for whom he provided intensive reading support almost always shot up in performance, making it easier to forgive his little heresies.

In some ways, Roger was a bit like Hiroo Onoda, the Japanese solider who hid himself in the jungles of a Philippine island until the 1970s, refusing to believe that World War II was over or that his side had lost. Over the past ten years, every state across the nation had come to accept the national Common Core standards, recognizing, it seemed, that concepts of algebra don't really change whether you're in North Dakota or North Carolina and that covalent bonds still work the same whether you're in Phoenix or Fairbanks. Like them or not, standards and their accompanying high-stakes tests were here to stay.

So were teacher performance measures and merit-pay provisions, like the ones Roger and his union holdout colleagues objected to— thanks in large part to the Obama administration's push for better measures of teacher performance, which had been fully enshrined with the passage of the All Children Exceeding Standards (ACES) Act in 2012.

Jasmine remembered a conference she had attended early in her teaching career, around 2009, during which a speaker called for an "education revolution." The speaker had insisted that the public education system was like a Rube Goldberg contraption, a needlessly complicated machine—for example, a bowling ball runs down an incline, hits an old boot, which, in turn, knocks over a paint can that releases a spring that shoots out a rubber ball to flip on a light switch. "We would never have consciously set out to build a system like this," the speaker insisted. "We should start over from scratch and build a better system, not based on what we already have, or what adults want, but what our kids *need*." The speaker didn't provide much detail about what the new system would look like, but Jasmine remembered the conference-goers around her getting really excited about some vague notion of creating schools that served the needs of every student, where kids could explore their own interests and learning was no longer restricted to the regular school day.

In the end, Jasmine felt that cooler heads had prevailed. Instead of "blowing up the system and starting over" or searching for some technology miracle that would "transform education as we know it," as some people at the conference had insisted, policymakers and reformers had taken a more measured approach, looking for ways to tweak and improve the existing educational system. While the Investing in Innovation (i3) fund had been intended to support the proliferation of radical new ideas that would transform education, in the end, the approaches it supported, like the Teach for America program, were not exactly breathtaking in their originality but nonetheless important improvements—sort of like software patches for a faulty programming code in the operating system of education. The results of these patches—clearer national standards, new approaches to recruiting and compensating teachers, and better data to guide improvement efforts—were significant and positive enough to restore people's faith in the public education system. At the same time, dwindling resources for education—thanks to the prolonged economic recession—also diminished the public's appetite for radical changes to public schools.

Outside Jasmine's eighth-grade classroom, students were in groups of two and three, most of them with their All-in-Ones around their wrists. How they could text so easily with one hand, Jasmine never could figure out, but at least they didn't have to haul around those heavy backpacks like she had to in high school. No backaches and slumped shoulders for these kids. Everything they needed was right around their wrists. Of course, they had to use the laptops at their desks in school. Eventually, she thought, maybe the school would catch up and get all of its software onto the All-in-Ones. That would help those kids who had trouble typing with two hands.

"Good morning!" Jasmine chirped brightly to the class. "Are we ready to go?" she asked, clapping her hands together.

"Bring it on," said a boy named Julius, his eyes beaming.

At an assembly yesterday, the principal, Mrs. Cheevers, had marched around the stage of the auditorium, seeming to channel some motivational speaker, encouraging the kids to shine on the test and "show the world what you've got."

The kids seemed to have taken the message to heart. They had shaken off the cobwebs of the adolescent-unfriendly hour of 8:30 a.m. and were now steeling themselves to respond to Mrs. Cheevers' challenge.

"Grab a laptop out of the bin and find a seat. It's that time of year again. You get to show your stuff to me and to the world. Power off the All-in-Ones. Let's get ready!"

After a few more prompts from Jasmine, the kids were all in their seats with a laptop. Jasmine used her own laptop to signal tech support that it was time to block all available wireless networks from the classroom with the exception of the one needed to administer the standardized exam. This assured that, even if students failed to power down their All-in-Ones as instructed, no external information would be available to them. Jasmine demonstrated on the interactive wall how to locate and open the icon for the test and then directed the students to begin.

Jasmine's mind wandered as she watched her students. She looked at Juan and hoped that Roger's recent reading interventions were going to make a difference today. She was so glad that his formative tracking caught the problems at home last month that were showing up in his classwork. She had taken his case to the Learning Forum, and together, they came up with an intervention that helped Juan's home situation and got him caught up. The new after-school program they had recently begun was a big help for Juan.

The Learning Forum was part of the school's intentional approach to early intervention for the students and to professional development for the teachers. Once a week, students were dismissed early so that teachers could work together to improve their practice using real-life problems and challenges that showed up each week on the students' progression reports. Jasmine hated to think what would have happened to Juan in the old days. He would probably have fallen off the radar and become one of the acceptable education casualties.

Finally, it was time for the lunch break. Jasmine signaled to the class to save their work, close their laptops, and break for lunch. As she went down the hall to grab her lunch from the lounge, she saw a group of parents in the community room discussing a proposed open-campus lunch policy. The school had always had a closed campus during lunch, and without a cafeteria, students had to bring their own food. But recently, gang violence in the neighborhood had diminished, and as the economy had improved, a number of new lunch spots had opened up nearby. Students, and some parents, wanted the school to consider opening the campus during lunch hour and letting the kids help out with the economic recovery of the neighborhood by buying meals off campus. Jasmine was glad that Mrs. Cheevers, the school's principal, could take care of issues like this and leave the teachers free to teach. Rita Cheevers trusted her teachers enough to not watch over their shoulders every day, but Jasmine knew that Rita kept a close watch on the kids' progression reports every week and would jump in if things got off track.

Rita, Jasmine's friend and longtime colleague, was in her early fifties and a force to be reckoned with. The daughter of a Jamaican community organizer, she displayed her father's firebrand passion for social justice. However, unlike her father, Roger, or many of the other old-guard teachers, Rita wasted no time wringing her hands about whether this system of education was the right one.

"My father used to complain about the system," Rita had told Jasmine in her lilting West Indian accent. "He worried about the powers that be giving children brainwash education and all of that." After her father died, her mother moved Rita and her siblings to, fittingly enough, Jamaica, New York, where Rita graduated near the top of her high school class before attending Miami University in Ohio.

"We're just two people," Rita told Jasmine one evening as they sat together in Rita's kitchen, planning their approach to the new school. "We could spend our lifetimes trying to change the system and never get anywhere. Meanwhile, hundreds, maybe thousands, of kids could slip past us, only to get chewed up by the system. What we *can* do is help them work the system," Rita had said, her voice growing loud in the way it did when she started to gear up for one of her hellfire-and-brimstone speeches, like the one she had given the day before the test to the school's students. "When you play basketball, you don't stop and complain about the rules, do you? You don't ask, 'Who came up with these rules? How come I can't dribble with both hands or shoot *three* free throws at a time?' No, you just learn the rules and try to play the game better than anyone else. That's how you win. Well, we're talking about a game here that's much more important than basketball. It's called life. And *this* . . . "—she thumped her temple with her finger— " . . . is how you win it. You've got to *learn*, children."

It was a simple message, one which the students at Bronx City Day took to heart.

As the day drew to a close, Jasmine told her students to finish the problem they were working on, save their work, and close their laptops. As the final laptop closed, the class let loose with a loud "hurrah!" As they stood up to stretch, each eighth-grader reached for his or her All-in-One and turned it back on. "If I didn't know better," thought Jasmine, "I'd think they were all checking the time!" But no, they were just powering up, beginning their networked lives again—smiling, laughing, happy to be back in touch with the rest of the world.

Jasmine said good-bye to her students and powered down her own laptop. As her students filed out of the room, she found herself thinking about Rita's words. Maybe it was all a game, but it had always been a game. At least now the rules were clear to everyone. And that meant that kids in the Bronx had almost as good a shot at doing well in it as kids anywhere.

Reflection Questions

Of the four scenarios presented in this book, this one is in many ways closest to our own current reality. As we noted earlier, though, it's unlikely that *nothing* will change in the future, so this scenario includes several significant changes from education as we know it. A key purpose of scenarios is to move us outside of our imagined future—the future as we *want* it to be—so that we might imagine other alternatives that prompt us to question some of our basic assumptions about what the future may hold. Hopefully, this scenario has accomplished that purpose.

We offer the following questions to help you consider—as an individual or as part of a study group—the implications of this scenario for yourself, your colleagues, your school, and your students.

1   Imagine that it is 2020 and that this scenario has unfolded in your school community. Picture yourself as successful in your profession and in this world. What specialized skills and resources did you bring with you from 2010 that contributed to your success in 2020? What specialized skills and resources have you acquired since 2010 that give you a decided edge in 2020?

2   If you were to see this scenario coming to fruition, what changes might you make in your own professional development or career choices?

3   Think about other education professionals you work with or hire. What skills, resources, and dispositions should they possess in order to be successful in this scenario? What will it take to make sure they retain or acquire these skills and resources by 2020?

4   Think about your school, district, or education organization. Is it prepared to survive in this world? Will it be sufficiently able to adapt to the changes envisioned in this scenario? What resources will it need to survive and thrive in this world? If this scenario begins to become reality, what changes should your organization begin to make? What should it start doing? What should it *stop* doing?

5   What skills will students need in order to be successful in this scenario? Of those skills, which ones are currently being taught in your setting? Which ones are missing or minimal? What is currently being taught in your setting that would likely be obsolete in the scenario?

6   What will it take to ensure that *every* child is successful in this future? Do you see challenges to the success of every child?

What has to happen, starting now and continuing through 2020, for every child to be successful in this scenario?

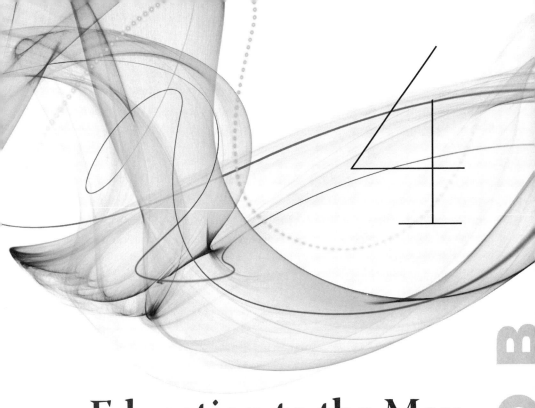

Education to the Max

This scenario depicts a future in which schools, districts, state agencies, and the other familiar trappings of the current educational system have survived intact in 2020. Just as they did in 2008 (Bushaw & Gallup, 2008), parents and the general public have continued to strongly support improving the current system of education rather than scrapping it and starting something new. However, the outcomes of education are now differentiated for each student, taking into account each child's unique talents, interests, and aptitudes, as well as the business community's need for a diversified workforce with a wide range of skills. In this scenario, NCLB has been replaced with a new law called the Maximize Every Child's Potential Act, promoting differentiated learning outcomes within a system of national accountability. This is a world of differentiated diplomas, strengths-based pedagogy, and individual learning plans for every student. In this world, success is measured literally one child at a time.

In this scenario, today's economic crisis has led the public to turn to government to tighten up regulations and get its house in order. As Wall Street and the economy have begun to recover, the public has regained some faith in the government's institutions, including public education. In addition, the Millennial generation has matured and become a powerful voting bloc. With their tendency to see government as part of the solution to social problems, they have added support to the notion of working to improve the current system rather than abandoning it. However, the failures of NCLB (which by 2010 had led to more than half of U.S. schools being identified as needing improvement) have led policymakers and the public to believe that equal treatment of *all* children in public education resulted in a system that institutionally failed to recognize the unique needs of *each* child and, as a result, served the needs of no one.

Deep Causes

As noted earlier, underlying every scenario are many key trends, or deep causes, that drive the future toward the outcomes depicted in the scenario. For this scenario, which lies in the differentiated/optimized quadrant of our matrix, we envision that several forces, including society's more favorable disposition toward government solutions, could serve to preserve the current system. At the same time, continued experience with web-based commerce offering a plethora of choices to consumers combined with the need for job security could lead parents and students to expect learning opportunities tailored to their children's learning needs, interests, and career aspirations. The following sections describe these drivers of change in more detail.

Economic Influences

The primary economic deep causes in this quadrant revolve around the economic meltdown and the pressure to prepare students for work and college. High job loss and unemployment rates define the economic environment. Evidence from a number of reports indicates the concern

of students, parents, and employers that high school and college graduates are not sufficiently prepared for the world of work (most notably,
American Diploma Project, 2004; Conference Board, Inc., Partnership
for 21st Century Skills, Corporate Voices for Working Families, &
Society for Human Resource Management, 2006).

In addition, concerns regarding *global competitiveness* indicate that
not only must students be ready to work or go to college, they must
possess higher-order skills, such as the ability to think critically, to
access and make sense of information, and to innovate in order to help
the United States compete on a global scale (most notably, National
Academy of Sciences, National Academy of Engineering, & Institute of
Medicine, 2007; National Center on Education and the Economy, 2008).
Several states have either started initiatives to address work- and college-
readiness or have joined with organizations such as the Partnership
for 21st Century Skills, Achieve, and States' Career Clusters Initiative.

In "Education to the Max," these economic and workforce-readiness
trends indicate continued support for federal involvement in education, which is viewed as part of the solution to the country's economic
troubles. Indeed, with the country's economy in decline, there is an
imperative to move quickly to ensure that *all* students graduate able
to contribute to the workplace in a productive way. There is no more
time to get it right; the economy cannot support students who drop
out or who graduate without the skills to be successful in work or college. As the trend continues to play out, education policymakers are
pressured to wed accountability to success for each and every student
in ways that the NCLB legislation failed to do. Differentiated pathways
through and out of school are seen as the solution. As the economy
recovers, public support for the new, improved system of education is
strengthened, and sustaining funds continue to flow.

No Child Left Behind

In this scenario, the failures of NCLB have taught education policymakers and the public that attempting to hold all schools to the same

standard when three-fourths of them are failing to meet that standard simply will not work. Furthermore, an educational system that loses 30 percent of its students before they graduate and graduates a large proportion of the remainder lacking the skills needed to successfully enter college or a career is clearly not fulfilling the promise that no child is left behind. However, NCLB was successful at using accountability to keep all children on the radar; thus, the accountability features of the law were retained while the strict mandates were discarded.

This perspective is supported by the Obama administration's stated position on NCLB, indicating that the government "should get 'tighter' about goals, insisting on more rigorous academic standards that are uniform across the states," and "giving folks more flexibility in how they achieve their goals" (Associated Press, 2009a). As this scenario unfolds, the flexibility provision reveals itself through greater reliance upon brain-based research and professional wisdom about how children learn.

In this quadrant, we hypothesize that these best practices, reflecting long-held beliefs of educators and demonstrated to work through stealth measures necessary under NCLB, are expanded through the effective use of education stimulus funds. The stimulus focus on data systems and college- and career-ready standards sets the groundwork for an educational system that promotes differentiated learning and outcomes within a system of national accountability.

The scenario assumes that the current delay in the reauthorization of NCLB continues and that, when the law is finally reauthorized, the tension existing today between "standardized" and "differentiated" outcomes for learning has been resolved in favor of more differentiated outcomes. This is in part due to the continuing failure of so many schools to achieve 100-percent proficiency under NCLB. Thus, NCLB is reframed as the Maximize Every Child's Potential Act (or "Max," as we conjecture it might be commonly called). Max retains the characteristics of national accountability for student achievement but recognizes that achievement is best measured student by student and that educational success requires maximizing the potential of every student.

National Standards

Another key driver for this quadrant is the tension between national standards and local control. The current administration, state governors, and influential policy groups are coming out in favor of "fewer, clearer, higher" standards to guide education, using the argument that educational success should look the same in Idaho as it does in Florida (Hoff, 2009). However, the discussion of national standards is not new and has run into trouble when standards are actually put on paper; states and interest groups just cannot agree, and so far, no coordinating effort has been able to overcome the differences (Hoff, 2009).

In addition, the business community has yet to firmly weigh in on whether they believe national standards, clearly designed to position all students for success in college, will properly prepare students for success in the workplace. No faction believes that all students *will* go to college. However, there is not yet a clear consensus that national academic standards will properly prepare those who elect to go from high school directly to the workforce. Business may become more forceful in the call for trade and career standards, and for evidence of students meeting those standards.

We hypothesize that legislation like "Max" could arise from the failure of the current Common Core initiative to create uniform standards across the U.S. In this scenario, it becomes too difficult for a critical mass of states to agree on the standards, and by the end of 2011, it is clear that the movement is going nowhere. This lack of consensus regarding what American students should know and be able to do leaves the door wide open to tackling the larger question that has been on the minds of educators for years and is prevalent in this quadrant's student-by-student philosophy: is it possible to answer the question "What should American students know and be able to do?" in the same way for all students?

However, it is reasonable to believe that, in an optimized system with public support for government involvement in education, a compromise is reached. Acknowledging the need for a common, foundational set of

standards appropriate for all students, national standards for education are developed and accepted up to a certain point; states aren't
willing to entirely cede their authority to self-determine educational
outcomes. However, there is little argument about what constitutes a
solid, foundational education for children ages three to nine. Thus, the
scenario envisions the National Basic Skills (NoBS) standards, passed
in 2012, as national common standards defining what all three- to
nine-year-olds should know in reading, communication, information
literacy, and mathematics. After that, states reinvent themselves with
models that push creativity and innovation, differentiation in approach,
and outcomes that lead to educational success.

Differentiated Pathways and Outcomes

This quadrant represents the view that uniform educational treatment of unique, dynamic individuals is inherently flawed and fails to
serve all students. Differentiated approaches and outcomes fit perfectly
with the educational philosophy of this quadrant, which holds that
since the days of segregation and tracking, the education pendulum has
swung too far in the other direction; in our fear of inequity, we have
created an educational system characterized by conformity and rigidity.

The current school-choice movement is probably a reflection of this.
Charter schools embody parental desires and visions for an education
that is different, better, or more suited to their children than the traditional neighborhood school. Parents who support choice will almost
certainly support differentiated outcomes, provided there is assurance
of equal quality across all outcomes.

In this scenario, Pathways and Outcomes are the defined skills-devel-
opment sets that determine coursework and the demonstrated learning
associated with differentiated outcomes. Pathways and Outcomes are
classified as those that lead to college and those that lead to careers, and
were developed in cooperation with relevant higher education and business partners. Schools employ EduLife coaches to counsel individual

students about their interests and aptitudes and the alignment of those with their progression through school along Pathways and Outcomes.

Use of ARRA Stimulus Funds

The ARRA economic stimulus package includes funds designated to improve statewide longitudinal data systems, as well as money to foster innovation to promote student achievement. While the specifics of these programs have not been released at the time of this writing, these funds could be used to advance programs that will ultimately support differentiated outcomes. In this scenario, the stimulus funds are used to legitimize and bring to scale some of the local mechanisms that states and districts have currently been implementing under NCLB: longitudinal data systems, academic programs targeted to specific groups and needs, and individualized learning plans (ILPs) for every student. With full funding and support, these programs prove to bring scalable benefits, reinforcing the differentiation necessary to maximize every child's potential.

Advances in Instruction and Assessment

This quadrant must be supported by new forms of instruction and assessment. Evidence of advances in this area adds plausibility to this scenario.

The Higher Education Act reauthorized in 2008 included a provision to establish a new National Center for Research in Advanced Information and Digital Technologies:

> The center will be charged with supporting research and development of new education technologies, including internet-based technologies. It will also help adapt techniques already widely used in other sectors, such as advertising and the military, to classroom instruction. For instance, the center could work on developing educational programs that use personalization, a technique used by Web sites such as Amazon. com to help hone consumers' individual preferences,

and simulation, which the military has used to help teach budding pilots how to fly planes. (Klein, 2008)

High-quality content must accompany personalization and simulation in the classroom. Online textbooks and, perhaps more relevant, open textbooks are increasingly available. Flat World Knowledge (www .flatworldknowledge.com) is pioneering open college textbooks, and traditional publishers, such as Pearson Scott Foresman, are sinking substantial money into developing multimedia capabilities. In a recent study, "80 percent of curriculum directors agreed that print and electronic textbooks would be replaced by a core digital curriculum in the next five years" (Dillon, 2008, p. 22). The digitization of curricula will facilitate differentiation within the classroom by providing the flexibility to customize content and utilize different ways to deliver that content.

Higher education has used an electronic portfolio system for some time. Paul Basken (2008), a writer for the *Chronicle of Higher Education*, reports,

> Hundreds of colleges use some type of electronic system for assembling and storing student work. But a few dozen, acting without federal direction and with little other outside coordination, have developed more sophisticated versions that guide assessment and curriculum development. They include both small institutions, such as Thomas College in Maine and Kapiolani Community College in Hawaii, and large ones, such as Minnesota's state colleges and the University of Washington. (p. 1)

While an electronic portfolio system is currently neither cheap nor easy to use, continued advancements are expected.

The expanded use of technology for differentiated learning, assessment, and instruction is being promoted by business (Intel, Microsoft, and Cisco Education Task Force, 2008), trade groups (Trotter, 2008), the U.S. Department of Education (2004), and the Consortium for School Networking.

The Scenario

This blog post and the responses following are excerpts from a public blog that has existed since 2011. The responses captured here have been placed in Smithsonipedia's permanent collection under Education History, as they highlight the political, environmental, and social turmoil the country was experiencing as education shifted from the 20th to the 21st century. Most notably, the original post and selected responses show the varying degrees of support as education moved from the NCLB Act to the Maximize Every Child's Potential (Max) Act.

As with most blogs, the writers use pseudonyms related to the positions they take in the dialogue. EdSkeptic generally takes a skeptical view of the reforms being discussed, while EduVator represents the innovative point of view, and so forth. The moderator initiates and maintains the discussion. This blog takes place in the course of one day.

Posted on Wednesday, October 28, 2020, at 7:25 a.m. by Moderator:

Only one week to go and this endless election season will be over. No matter the outcome, on the education front, I'm going to start lobbying the ed crowd immediately to make sure that Max is left alone. Even though Max was passed as a bipartisan piece of legislation, if the White House changes parties in this election, who knows what will happen. I surely don't want to go back to NCLB. Max is solid. Hands off.

Posted on Wednesday, October 28, 2020, at 8:13 a.m. by EdSkeptic:

Oh, please. Max is a bigger dog than Bo, for cripes' sake. Max was a transparent Democratic ploy to put their stamp on education before Obama's popularity wore off. Obama and the Dems in Congress knew they had to act fast before the chickens came home to roost with healthcare reform and deficit spending. When they reauthorized NCLB and repackaged it as Max, they did a horrible injustice to poor kids across the country. This law is just segregation in disguise. We all know that poor kids get put into non-college tracks more than rich white kids do. "*Max*imize Every Child's Potential," "Education to the *Max*," "*Max*" . . .

call it whatever you want, it's been around ten years and needs to go out with the rest of the trash.

Posted on Wednesday, October 28, 2020, at 8:37 a.m. by Moderator:

EdSkeptic, you need to revisit your American history hyperlink. "Horrible injustice to poor kids," you say? Max helped those kids! We have national accountability for student achievement; after the debacle in the financial industry that brought on the Great Recession, we learned our lessons about oversight. The most recent Max reauthorization added the provision that all three- to nine-year-olds had to show a year's progress in the NoBS standards. That closed the last loophole that perpetuated the achievement gap. The latest accountability summary shows that kids are represented almost equally across Pathways and Outcomes that lead to college and Pathways and Outcomes that lead to careers when disaggregated by socioeconomic status.

Max was meant to correct the horrible injustice of 30 percent dropouts, of unemployable graduates, and of college remediation, and has done just that. Your argument is old and tired.

Posted on Wednesday, October 28, 2020, at 9:19 a.m. by EduVator:

Hold on. I remember getting that big bag of stimulus money right after Obama was elected to his first term and being ordered to "innovate." From my perspective, Max was the result of the hard work we did at the state and local levels with the stimulus money—and then the sustaining money—to improve our data and assessment systems. We always *knew* that kids in our schools needed to be monitored individually. And all that brain-based research (Gardner, 2004; Medina, 2008) going on at the time just reinforced what we had known all along. Those of us actually in education knew that kids should be taught, assessed, and monitored individually, but, as usual, we were the last to be asked.

The stim gave us the means to "innovate" our way out from under the oppressive accountability of NCLB and advance what we knew to be good practice. Max wouldn't have the Pathways and Outcomes provision today if it weren't for those of us already in education pushing the notion that we would be accountable to outcomes if we could just customize education for individual kids. The EduLife coach at my school just got back from training where he learned about revisions to the Geoscaper (Social Technologies, 2007) diploma certification requirements. And my kinesthetic teachers [referring to teachers assigned to learners strong in kinesthetic intelligence, one of Gardner's (2004) identified intelligences] went to a professional development session to learn new research on activating different brain areas through movement so they can help their science students learn faster and retain more. Those of us in education led the parade for differentiation with accountability. Where do you think the tagline "Success is measured one child at a time" came from?

Posted on Wednesday, October 28, 2020, at 9:47 a.m. by Moderator:

EduVator, I remember that stim money, too. I have to point out, though, that the child-by-child accountability outlined in Max wouldn't be possible (or would at least be a lot harder) if Microsoft and ACT hadn't teamed up to build PREPARE (Proprietary Electronic Portfolio Assessment and Reporting Environment). Without it, you'd never know how well your kids were lining up against the NoBS standards and the Pathways and Outcomes. And it's a good thing, too, that ACT adapted their assessments for aptitude and interest. I'll admit that your use of the stim money got things started, but Max is what kept the sustaining financial incentives flowing after the stim was gone. I'm not sure all this would have worked without the technology to support it. Good thing they saw the writing on the wall and followed the money.

Posted on Wednesday, October 28, 2020, at 11:12 a.m. by IHeartPolicy:

While I agree with the education folks giving themselves a pat on the back, Max wouldn't have wings if not for policy pressure. I was a staffer for the NGA in the late 2010s, and I remember the whole push to bring America up to speed with global education and global economic competition. Arne Duncan (Obama's first secretary of ed) implemented the NoBS standards before he left in 2012, largely because of policy pressure resulting from the NGA's international benchmarking project with CCSSO and Achieve. When you looked at it on paper, the U.S. came up short across the board, so the policy pressure to reform education got intense. We know now that was the intent of the NGA project all along. It takes Congress to pass laws, but it takes political pressure to move mountains. Of course, we will approach the new administration with an open mind, but the International Skills and Competencies Benchmarks (ISCB) components of Max aren't going anywhere.

Posted on Wednesday, October 28, 2020, at 11:29 a.m. by Moderator:

IHeartPolicy, glad to hear we can count on your support to protect Max! We need to stress how Max has helped our global position. I'd stay away from the data about trade and manufacturing. We need to focus instead on how our kids have moved up in design and innovation, and how that's helping us in nanotechnology, entertainment, and PCDs [personal communication devices].

Posted on Wednesday, October 28, 2020, at 12:26 p.m. by EduCitizen:

I thought Max was a response to the economy. I remember those dark days of 2011, when the market *really* tanked. We didn't have time to namby-pamby around, letting kids "discover" themselves while they dropped out and sponged off the system. Kids needed to get through school and get a job, or go to college and start filling their brains with things that would make the country money. Max was supposed to stop the bleeding caused by all those NCLB kids who dropped out or graduated with no real ability to work or learn. And it did! I used to hire kids out of high school, and even out of college, who couldn't show up to work on time and couldn't read a technical manual or write a status report to save their lives. My trade association helped build those Pathways and Outcomes, and now, when a kid shows up with an industry certification on his diploma, I *know* what I'm getting. No more pig in a poke. And my own son, who wanted to get in to MIT so he could take over the old man's business someday and "take it global," knew exactly what he had to do every step of the way to get his MIT ticket punched when he graduated.

Posted on Wednesday, October 28, 2020, at 1:04 p.m. by Moderator:

EduCitizen, good point. We should never forget (as if we could) the slap in the face education received in the midst of the Great Recession. The college/work-ready movement got a huge push after the crash. I think it was like the "dust bowl" days of the Great Depression—everything came down to a matter of survival. I like to think about those times as when we really found out what we were made of. You're right—no more namby-pamby. We took kids' natural strengths and interests and used the educational system to amplify them rather than squash them under an avalanche of classes to make them "well rounded." Graduation rates today are around 90 percent (of course, the cutbacks in unemployment and welfare contribute to that, too). I'm proud that we've returned to our heritage, where you carry your own weight. I guess it took the Great Recession for us to pull together and find our American strength again. Did you hear the Chinese minister of education last month when he spoke at the ISCB meeting? He knows that we are formidable and that no one can match our educational system for spawning innovation. They might be able to out-produce us, but they'll never out-innovate us.

Posted on Wednesday, October 28, 2020, at 2:22 p.m. by AngryEngineer:

They will never out-innovate us because of the Great Rebellion (that's what I call it, anyway) against the false promises of book learning. We, the disenfranchised book-smart, bought into an educational system that promised us opportunity in exchange for studying science and math from books and old professors. Too late, we realized that the education and book learning stressed in the early 2000s as the pathway to assured jobs in the global economy was completely disconnected from the demands and expectations of future employers. Instead, we should have received more in the way of creative problem solving, creativity, design, innovation . . . the right-brain strengths that were neglected under the left-brain focus of teaching and testing. *We* partnered with the business community to demand retraining, and reinforced the reformation of education to brain-based, differentiated outcomes that feed the needs of business and higher education.

Posted on Wednesday, October 28, 2020, at 2:45 p.m. by MyThreeSons:

I have to add to what AngryEngineer said. I have three sons who have gone through school, each marching to the tune of the day. It sounds like my oldest went through with AngryEngineer; he did what he was told he needed to do in order to succeed. Unlike AngryEngineer, though, my son didn't really want to go to college. He wanted to become a master carpenter. His father and I talked to the school counselors and were told that all students had to be prepared to go to college, whether they actually wanted to go to college or not. We were assured that the skills were the same. Well, my older son graduated from high school completely unprepared to get a job in the trades. My middle son went through a differentiated school program after the Max law. He also didn't want to go to college; he wanted to become a chef. Under the differentiated program, math and reading were integrated into his culinary coursework. He honed his math skills converting metric measurements and learned a lot of French from studying cuisine. He was so happy to go to school every day. He is a sous-chef at a New York restaurant now. My third son is just finishing up high school, and he *does* want to go to college. He's been working with admissions at UC Berkeley since his freshman year in high school. It is my observation that once schools stopped trying to force-fit college on every kid, the kids got out of school much better prepared to do their thing and were much happier in school while they were there.

Posted on Wednesday, October 28, 2020, at 3:10 p.m. by Moderator:

AngryEngineer and MyThreeSons, I'm getting a little humbled by all the times I've had to say "you're right" today. The government gave birth to it, and it's up to us to protect it, but I guess it's fair to say, looking at the discussion posts today, that it really took a village to raise Max.

Under Max, people recognized the value of the trades, of skilled craftsmen—good-paying jobs that don't require a college degree and that we couldn't lose overseas. What we did as a country was get off our high horse and see that not every kid needs to go to college. Right now, the jobs with the highest levels of career satisfaction and job security are in the trades. Our colleges are catching up through design and innovation, but without Max, your middle son would have been lost.

Posted on Wednesday, October 28, 2020, at 3:22 p.m. by IToldYouSo:

I've been reading along, and I have to say, I just don't get it. My granddaughter gave me this new laptop because all the newspapers are going out of print. She said I could keep up with the news. But it sure seems to me that you all don't really know what you're talking about. All these problems you are talking about were *caused* by the government butting into our business! And here you all are talking about how the government is fixing education. *Laws* don't fix problems; *people* do. Modern education is in a heap of trouble. The only way it will get better is if we stop looking to those who caused the problem to fix it.

Posted on Wednesday, October 28, 2020, at 4:00 p.m. by Moderator:

IToldYouSo, you bring up a point that I hear a lot from the older crowd. We're going to have to agree to disagree on this one, because we see things very differently. The financial meltdown, wasted billions in misspent war money, a national debt in the trillions . . . these were *not* caused by a government that was "too involved." The country's problems were caused by a lack of oversight, by social institutions run amok. Sure, too much government is a pain in the pocket and can get in the way, but too little government isn't the answer, either.

Education reformers tried it the other way in the early 2010s. The "blow it up and start over" education reform crowd was convinced that the system was broken and started a movement to reinvent schooling. The result for those unfortunate guinea pigs was a free-for-all: no structure; nobody knew what anybody was learning; the "haves" took power, and the "have nots" were excluded . . . that ship sank faster than the *Titanic*, with just as many casualties.

We saw the alternative to the current system, and it was ugly. Our system isn't perfect, but it's better than the alternative. If I may be permitted to speak for my generation for a moment, I would say that we have been left with the residue from "free market" policies, and we just don't buy the argument that it's all the government's fault. We're fine with the notion that the government is our partner to solve the problems we were left with. We're going to do right by our kids, and if the government can help us fix the education mess, then we're on board.

Posted on Wednesday, October 28, 2020, at 4:25 p.m. by PhilOSopher:

With apologies to the Bard, this whole debate appears to be "full of sound and fury, signifying nothing." We're arguing over the merits of a piece of legislation without considering the real purpose of education. Many of the comments here seem to suggest that education is really just glorified job training, as if the only thing that matters in life is collecting a steady paycheck. Socrates once said, "The unexamined life is not worth living." So, too, an unexamined education is not worth learning. We should be teaching our children how to become careful thinkers who examine their own assumptions and those handed down by authority figures—including their teachers and their elected officials.

Another great mind, Thomas Jefferson, wrote, "If a nation expects to be ignorant and free, in a state of civilization, it expects what never was and never will be." In the name of global competitiveness and our zeal to "keep up" with undemocratic nations, we have perpetrated on our youth a shallow, shortsighted form of learning that does nothing to preserve the core values of our nation or democracy.

I agree with AngryEngineer to some extent—not all learning should be book learning, but the purpose of developing students' critical thinking abilities isn't merely to help us out-innovate the Chinese, but also to create a new generation of great minds to help humanity solve some of its most intractable problems, while at the same time helping all students find meaning in this life, which is, to return to Shakespeare, all too quickly extinguished, like a "brief candle."

Posted on Wednesday, October 28, 2020, at 4:40 p.m. by Moderator:

Whoa, PhilOSopher, those are some deep thoughts there. On one level, I agree with you as I can assure you that my own college degrees in sociology and English were anything *but* job training. I graduated with a head full of ideas under my mortarboard and *no* marketable skills. My college experience—a broad, free-ranging exploration of ideas—was a great thing for me, even if it did leave me eating Top Ramen throughout much of my twenties. Yet while it was a great thing for *me*, I wouldn't wish it upon everyone. During my lean years, I had a financial safety net: my parents. Others aren't so fortunate. What Max has allowed students to do is select their own path—whether it's one that encourages deep self-examination or the more immediate rewards of a job that puts food on the table and money in the bank. Sure, people like you and me would love to have more people walking around with whom we can discuss Nietzsche and play Scrabble, but we shouldn't foist our own omphaloskepsis (that's a thirty-point Scrabble word!) on others.

Reflection Questions

Each successive scenario in this book pulls us a little farther from our current reality and perhaps our comfort zones. In this scenario, the educational system itself has avoided any dramatic, seismic shifts and upheavals. Yet this scenario envisions a world in which we have set dramatically new purposes and goals for education. Below are some questions to help you consider—as an individual or as part of a study group—the implications of this scenario for yourself, your colleagues, your school, and your students.

1   Imagine that it is 2020 and you are successful in your profession. What specialized skills, resources, and dispositions did you bring with you from 2010 that contributed to your

success in 2020? What specialized skills and resources have you acquired to give you an edge in a world in which the system has remained intact, focusing on ongoing, incremental improvements, yet its outcomes have become differentiated for individual students?

2 If you were to see this scenario coming to fruition, what changes might you make in your own professional development or career choices?

3 Think about other education professionals you work with or hire. What skills and resources should they possess in order to be successful in this scenario? What will it take to make sure they retain or acquire these skills and resources by 2020?

4 Think about your school, district, or education organization. Is it prepared to survive in this world? Will it be sufficiently able to adapt to the changes envisioned in this scenario? What resources will it need to survive and thrive in this future? If this scenario begins to become reality, what changes should your organization begin to make? What should it start doing? What should it *stop* doing?

5 What skills will students need in order to be successful in this scenario? Of those skills, which ones are currently being taught in your setting? Which ones are missing or minimal? What is currently being taught in your setting that would likely be obsolete in the scenario?

6 What will it take to ensure that *every* child is successful in this scenario? Do you see challenges to the success of every child? What has to happen, starting now and continuing through 2020, for every child to be successful in this scenario?

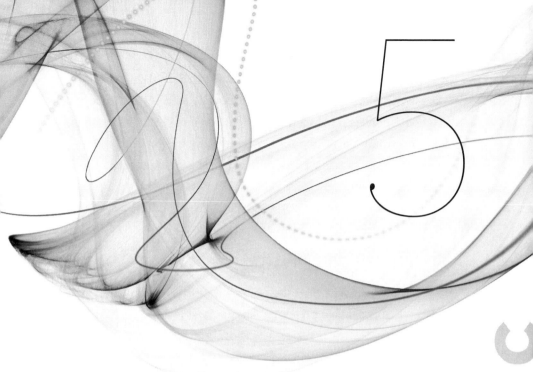

Who Killed Buster
the Bearcat?

This scenario describes a future in which educational technology—specifically, online schooling—has proven to be a disruptive innovation, transforming education as dramatically as digital music altered the music industry in the first years of the 21st century. In addition, a long, deep economic recession has made funding of the venerable school-based educational model unsustainable, leaving traditional classrooms vulnerable to takeover by savvy online learning providers. However, while the *delivery* of education has been reinvented, the *outcomes* have remained constant—rigidly fixed to a regimen of national assessments that track students' progress against their national (and international) peers, turning students and parents into shrewd consumers of those programs that best prepare them to succeed on the tests.

In this scenario, Jim Hughes, Winesburg High School class of 2009, returns to his alma mater only to find it bearing little resemblance to the school he once knew. After a stroll down memory lane with some fellow alums, Jim decides to investigate the reasons for the school's transformation from a typical suburban teenage enclave of forty-five-minute rotating, single-subject classes to a shopping mall–like cornucopia of online tutorials on such subjects as robotics. The school lacks anything resembling classrooms, and students come and go only to take assessments or for art or gymnastics classes. There is also an unusual focus on international rankings, namely a dreaded test that we envision being called the International Assessment of Educational Progress. It appears that policy, economics, and technology have all conspired to cause the transformation of the school and, ultimately, even the demise of the school's lovable mascot, Buster the Bearcat.

Deep Causes

Underlying this scenario, which lies in the standardized/reinvented quadrant of our matrix, are several key trends, including an ongoing economic slump, a decline in government funds, and a rise of cheaper online alternatives to schooling, that ultimately bring school districts to their knees. At the same time, political forces conspire to maintain a relentless focus on standards and standardized testing. The following sections describe these drivers of change in more detail.

Education Policy

In this scenario, federal policymakers continue with the same straight-line reform agenda they've been on since the 1990s, deciding that the best way to foster education innovation is to hold the desired outcomes constant while giving educators greater freedom to innovate and experiment. Indeed, in many ways, this vision for education is consistent with many early proponents of "new accountability," who called for more focus on education outputs and less red tape and regulation of inputs.

A Protracted Economic Downturn

The radical transformation of models of schooling envisioned in this scenario is brought about by the need to drastically reduce the costs of education, which are precipitated by a protracted economic downturn. This economic downturn could have several deep causes, including the inability of the U.S. economy to pull itself out of the economic slump caused by the bursting of the housing and credit bubble. Several trends or events might prolong the crisis, including rising costs of oil, rising costs of entitlement and health-care spending that create a drag on the economy, or a bubble (and subsequent bursting of that bubble) in the dollar and treasury bills caused by federal deficits and debt. In this scenario, it is this third possibility that results in a "lost decade" for the U.S. economy.

In this scenario, a black swan event has occurred. Foreign investors' flight from the U.S. dollar and bonds has restricted the U.S. government's ability to support many programs, including education, and created a long-term economic decline, reminiscent of the Great Depression.

Computer-Based Learning as a "Disruptive Innovation"

The third key deep cause of this scenario draws heavily from the 2008 book *Disrupting Class: How Disruptive Innovation Will Change the Way the World Learns*, in which Clayton Christensen and his colleagues predict that a "breathtaking flip" in how education is provided is likely to occur over the next ten years (p. 100). They base this prediction on the notion that disruptive innovations have, in the past, rapidly transformed entire industries—such as the way mp3 players and digitally downloaded music transformed the music business in less than a decade or the way that mail-order DVDs and on-demand cable programming led to the rapid demise of video rental stores.

Although the number of students enrolled in online courses remains relatively small, the number is growing exponentially. In 2000, just forty-five thousand students were engaged in online learning. By 2007, there were twenty-two times as many students learning online—fully one million. If this exponential curve continues—supported perhaps by continued advances and declining costs for bandwidth and display technologies—Christensen et al. project that, by the year 2018, about half of all high school courses will be delivered online.

The Scenario

Last summer, twelve hours into my annual visit with my parents in Ohio, I posted a desperate plea on my Facebook page: "Calling all Winesburg H.S. 2009 grads . . . is anyone still in town? Can't . . . talk . . . about . . . parents' . . . cholesterol levels . . . anymore. Will be at Shenanigans at 8 p.m. Please, please join me."

Thankfully, my Facebook post caught the attention of four former friends from school: two guys with whom I used to play baseball, a guy I sat next to for four years in homeroom, and a girl I worked with on the yearbook staff (who's now a woman, of course, and married to one of my former teammates). At some point in the evening, the conversation turned to the demise of our old school, Winesburg High. Feeling a little punchy, we went out to the tavern's back patio and poured our drinks on the ground in mock homage to our "homie," Buster the Bearcat—the mascot of our alma mater. As the evening wore on, we began to ponder, with a little more seriousness, just what exactly had happened to Buster . . . and the school we'd called home for four years.

Hey, Oh, Where'd You Go, Ohio?

Winesburg High School, like thousands of other high schools around the nation, no longer exists. The building is still there, but today it's called the Winesburg Learning Center. I discovered this the morning after I met my friends in the tavern, when I fled my parents' house yet again after my father's forty-five-minute rant on the vicissitudes of blood pressure.

When I arrived on the old campus, I was blown away by what I saw. For starters, it was summer, yet the building bustled with activity. The wing of the building where I took math classes was now called the Winesburg Testing Center. Inside what used to be Mr. Townsend's and Mrs. Rollins' classrooms—where I took algebra II and trigonometry—teenage kids sat in front of a bank of glowing monitors that surrounded the perimeter of the room. Their fingers danced away on tactile pads while a pair of testing proctors paced the room with their hands behind their backs, giving everyone the eagle eye. A sign on the wall warned about the penalties (up to thirty days in jail!) associated with cheating on tests given at the center. A sign on the door read, NO UBERUBI DEVICES PERMITTED BEYOND THIS POINT.

I went upstairs to what had been the old language arts hallway and found that it was now the Winesburg Tutoring Center. The whole floor had been converted into a bunch of high-walled cubicles in which adult tutors were working with students, sitting beside them as they plowed their way through online courses and practice tests. The place had the feel of a hair salon. A girl with a bouncy ponytail stood at a counter in the middle of the room and asked me if I had an appointment when I walked in.

"What happened to Ms. T's English classroom?" I asked her.

She blinked at me for a couple seconds with a confused look on her face until I explained that I was a visitor from the ancient past, the Winesburg High class of 2009. She said that the whole second floor of my old school had been leased to a privately run tutoring center. The tutors, many of them former teachers, had all been prescreened by the guy who runs the place (he also owns a car wash in town) "to make sure they're really smart and not criminals or anything like that," she explained.

In one corner of the room, kids were wearing headphones and speaking foreign languages into microphones, wincing occasionally when their computer tutors informed them that they'd mispronounced a word or misconjugated a verb. I also spotted a few kids interacting with tutors, not directly, but through their monitors.

"What's your weather like down there?" one kid asked his tutor. Judging by the kid's envious reaction, his tutor seemed to be dispensing advice from some beachside location.

Downstairs in the lobby of the school, where our trophy case had once sat, there was now a large screen that listed what at first I thought were high scores from a video game. But when I looked at them closer, I saw that they were local high scores on the International Assessment of Educational Progress. Apparently, there are some pretty smart cookies back in Winesburg: one kid ranked first statewide on some mathematics assessment, twenty-first nationwide, and in the top one hundred internationally.

In the courtyard outside the cafeteria, sitting on the wall where, in my day, seniors used to hang out and harass underclassmen as they scurried by on their way to class, a few high school–aged kids were doing some last-minute cramming before taking a proctored online trigonometry exam.

"Where are all your friends?" I asked them. "You know, when I was in high school, this place used to be crawling with teenagers."

"They're mostly at home," explained a kid who looked to be about fifteen. He wore his jeans in the new fashion—pulled snugly to his waist and cuffed at the bottom, like he'd just walked out of a 1950s black-and-white TV show.

I asked them how often they came to the building. Hardly ever, most of them said. They took nearly all of their classes online at home.

"I haven't gone to school, I mean, *really* gone to school, like day in and day out, since eighth grade," said one boy. Apart from a completely different sense of fashion—he was sporting a '50s throwback crew cut and a plaid shirt—it sounded like his elementary and middle school experience was more like my own. From kindergarten through eighth grade, he had spent his days inside a regular brick-and-mortar building with teachers, books, field days, hamsters, and awkward prepubescent cafeteria dances—basically, the whole nine yards. "But by the time I got to eighth grade, a lot of stuff we were doing was on computers," he explained.

By high school, attendance had become optional for these kids—as long as they kept their test scores up. There were no more bus rides. No more pep rallies. No more prom.

"Don't you miss hanging out with your friends?" I asked them.

"No, I mean, I chat with them online all the time," said one kid. "And there's a study group in my neighborhood clubhouse. And one over at the public library. I go there if I start feeling stir-crazy. The only reason anyone comes *here* . . ."—his voice was dripping with disdain for my old school—"is to take a test."

"Or if they don't have a good enough system at home or need some kind of special software or something like that," another kid added. He wore a pair of *Leave It to Beaver* Converse canvas high-top basketball shoes with rubber toes.

"Except for art. It's kind of hard to do pottery online," said a girl; she wore a skirt and the same bouncy ponytail as the girl I'd seen upstairs in the tutoring center. "Of course, that's not really *high school*," she added, pointing across the courtyard to what, back in my day, we called the fine arts annex. On the outside wall of the annex, where my school's motto had once been posted (something about being a better bearcat every day), now hung a sign that read, "Winesburg Community Center for the Arts."

"I've got a lot of old people in my pottery class," the girl continued. "They're nice. Sometimes they help me with my pots and stuff since they know I'm taking the class for credit. Most of them are just taking it for fun—to make Christmas presents for their grandkids."

"My parents *make* me come here," said one boy, who was hardly able to hide his disgust. Some things never change, I guess. "They both work and think I'm not focused enough to work at home by myself without someone bird-dogging me. It *is* kind of distracting at home, I guess," he confessed.

One girl said her gymnastics club practices in the gym, so she goes to that part of the campus a few times a week, but she is hardly ever in the main building. I asked if her team was called the Bearcats. She looked at me strangely and asked, "What's a bearcat?" Apparently, her gymnastics club rents the gym three days a week.

"My robotics class meets over there," added another kid, pointing in the direction of what used to be the auto mechanics class. The only robot he had at home just vacuumed the floor, grousing in chirps and blips when it ran into misplaced furniture; he got to work on *way* cooler robots in his robotics class. He said he came to school for tutoring in biology, before quickly adding, "I mean, I'm not *dumb* or anything like that. Right now, I'm at the eighty-second percentile—eighty-seventh nationwide. But I need to score higher than that, probably around the ninetieth percentile, to get into a good college pre-med program."

"It's a good thing you don't live in China," his friend pointed out.

"Yeah, then I'd be at, like, the twentieth percentile nationwide," he said, exaggerating a bit, I assumed. "But it's too bad I don't live in some backwards Podunk state; I'd be a total *genius* there." He proceeded to rattle off five states where he knew his current scores would put him well above the ninetieth percentile in biology—and nearly every other subject. "But I want to be a dentist," he explained. "And I don't think people in those states have all that many teeth."

I tried to share a few "back in my day" experiences with them, but I could tell they were on the verge of giving me that same eye-rolling "you're so unhip" look that I give my dad when he insists on calling his UberUbi an "Uber-Ubiquitous device," or worse, a BlackBerry—like he's just time-travelled from 2010.

Leaving quickly, to avoid inciting the kids' ridicule, I walked back out through the front doors of the school. As I left, I remembered poor old Buster and turned to see if his likeness was still emblazoned on the brick wall above the building's main entrance. All that remained of Buster was a faint pattern of discoloration in the bricks: a bearcat silhouette with one paw raised. Alas, Buster was gone.

On the way back to my parents' house, I found myself returning to the question that my friends and I had pondered the night before: what *had* happened in the eleven intervening years since I had left that turned Winesburg High, home of the mighty Bearcats (and three thousand teenagers), into the Winesburg Learning Center, a "come and go as you please" test-prep center on computerized steroids?

As someone who had once aspired to teach high school, I found myself intrigued by this mystery—a mystery that has no doubt been repeated in countless towns across America but which, for me, came down to a simple question: who killed Buster the Bearcat? After spending the next three months sleuthing for an answer, I have narrowed my list of suspects to three.

Suspect #1: Republicrats

I started my investigation by asking a bunch of (mostly former) educators what had made education change so rapidly. Many of them leapt to politics. The Democrats I talked to blamed the Republicans for commercializing education, turning it into, in their words, a "cold," "harsh," business-like system, where kids sat like "automatons" all day, clicking their way through standardized computer-based learning modules. The Republicans I spoke with blamed the Democrats for "socializing" education, steamrolling over time-honored traditions, such as local school boards, and letting bureaucrats in far-off Washington decide what kids learn.

When I probed more deeply, asking *specifically* what the Democrats or Republicans had done to transform—or in the words of some, "undermine"—education so dramatically, I was surprised by the answer. Democrats said that the Republicans had pushed relentlessly for national standards, high-stakes testing, and school choice. When I asked Republicans what the Democrats had done, I heard *the same thing*: they had pushed relentlessly for national standards, high-stakes testing, and school choice.

People on both sides blamed something called the Race to the Top program for ushering in national standards and tests while at the same time creating a "blow it up and start over" approach to school reform, which led to a lot of schools, like my alma mater, being essentially closed down and replaced with online learning facilities.

Sometimes I just have to sit back and admire politicians. Despite the partisan rancor, the two parties have spent the past thirty years moving in the same direction, at least on education issues, but blaming the other side for the policies their constituents don't like. Clearly, if you're looking for someone to pin Buster's murder on, the "Republicrats" have had the *opportunity* to commit the crime, as they've enjoyed uninterrupted one-party rule for the past thirty years.

Suspect #2: Black Swan Monday

The second suspect in my lineup is "Black Swan Monday." I'm sure we all remember where we were when we learned that foreign investors, like a frightened flock of birds, got spooked about the solvency of the U.S. government and fled the dollar en masse. How strange it was to wake up on the morning of October 15, 2012, and learn that while we were sleeping, the black swan event—the event no one thought possible until they actually saw it—had occurred, leaving the dollar bills in our wallets and bank accounts nearly worthless. I remember I woke that morning to a phone call from my father, who told me that I would need to find a way to pay my own way through college because his life savings had vanished overnight. "I should've listened to Buffett," he said ruefully.

"Warren or Jimmy?" I asked.

"Warren," he replied, not much in the mood for humor. "But maybe now that my money's all gone, I'll just listen to Jimmy."

If there's been one upside to life after Black Swan Monday, it's that we've learned as a nation how to be much more frugal—with everything from the homes in which we live (two of my old friends from Winesburg said they're living in homes with three generations under one roof) to the cars we drive (remember when two- and even three-car garages were insufficient for a family's fleet of wheels?) to how we approach education spending.

Let's face it, in the past, we weren't always getting the biggest bang for our education buck. At one time, we ranked *third* in the world in our investment in K–12 education, behind only Switzerland and Luxembourg, but *below* average on most measures of student performance when compared with thirty other developed nations (Organisation for Economic Co-operation and Development, 2008). In short, we were paying far *more* and getting far *less* for our education dollars than everyone else in the world.

Why was that? Well, in the name of local control, we insisted on "reinventing the wheel" in all fifty states and all fifteen thousand of the nation's school districts. Altogether, states spent three-quarters of a billion dollars creating their own assessment systems (Toch, 2006); districts spent another $10 billion on textbooks (Jackson, Burdt, Bassett, & Stein, 2004) and 3–4 percent of their operating budgets on administrative costs (including busing, groundskeeping, and building maintenance), which packed on another $20 billion in spending (Odden, Monk, Nakib, & Picus, 1995). The biggest expense, by far, though, was teachers. At their peak, there were nearly 3.8 million teachers nationwide. Some of them, like my tenth-grade American literature teacher, Ms. T, were *amazing*; you couldn't pay them enough. Other teachers, like Mr. B, who slipped out of school every day three minutes prior to the last bell to avoid getting stuck in the parking lot, were *terrible*; you couldn't show *them* the broom fast enough. Yet they all kept their jobs and got paid nearly the same salary.

Despite all of the head-scratching anachronisms and inefficiencies built into the old system, local control was seen as a constitutional right, an intractable "third rail" of education that no one would dare touch. However, like a lot of other cherished traditions, we reconsidered all of that when the dollar crashed and the cogs of our economy seized up.

Necessity, as they say, is the mother of invention. Over the past decade, as we were forced to reduce education spending, we turned to online learning and free-market mechanisms, like vouchers and tax credits, to cut the costs of education nearly in half. In the crucible created by Black Swan Monday, many of our time-honored (and anachronistic) education traditions, like assuming that the only way to teach teenagers is to corral them together in the same building for 180 days a year for four years, quickly burned away.

Suspect #3: Your UberUbi

The UberUbi device you're probably staring at as you read this column is, in a business sense, a serial killer. Along with its partner in crime, "Webinomics," the UberUbi device (and the iPhone before it, and the personal computer before those) led to the demise of your neighborhood video store and the music store in your shopping mall. When it finished off those institutions, it took aim at professionals, including many (nontrial) lawyers, realtors, and accountants, quickly replacing many of them with web tools. With similar speed, the creative destruction of web learning burned through education like a forest fire. In just ten years, computer-based learning went from something on the fringe of education to its mainstay, with almost every kid about age ten and up across the country spending anywhere from 50 to nearly 100 percent of his or her time learning in front of a computer.

I read recently about "the biggest teen idol you've never heard of"—a science teacher from Nebraska named Colt Atkins. He teaches nearly one hundred thousand teenagers through his caffeine-fueled lectures on—of all topics—physics. I was so intrigued that I called up the company to see if I could take a look at one of them. They graciously let me log into the module *pro gratis*. My mind was *blown*. Honestly, I found myself wishing I were back in high school, learning from Mr. Atkins. Who knows . . . had I spent a year with him instead of Mr. B, I might have become an astrophysicist instead of a starving freelance writer (and author of three unpublished mystery novels).

Allow me to insert a personal aside: while sleuthing, I got in touch with my old teacher Ms. T. She told me that she was designing American literature classes for a big online course provider. Some of her lessons are now viewed by fifty thousand kids nationwide. I think she's also making some pretty good coin, which makes me immensely happy. I asked her about good old Mr. B. She told me that he's now a parking lot attendant at the Columbus airport. Ironic justice there.

I told Ms. T that I was working on a mystery about Buster the Bearcat. She reminded me that every good mystery needs a surprise ending. I assured her I wouldn't disappoint.

Hercule Poirot Reveals the Killer

This is the part of the mystery where I call all of the suspects into the room to confront them with their crime. Cue the ominous cellos while I point to the strange-looking half-donkey/half-elephant in one corner of the room and offer my first theory of who killed Buster. As I anticipated, each half of the Republicrat blames the other for the crime. Then I turn to the black swan, which tries to gobble up the last few incriminating crumbs of U.S. dollars on its beak. Then I wheel around and expose the dark deeds of your UberUbi device, which has coolly donned a mini aquarium screen saver. But in the end, I announce that no single one of these suspects actually killed Buster. Rather, like the final twist in *Murder on the Orient Express* (thank you, Ms. T, for turning me on to Agatha Christie), all *three* suspects collaborated to kill Buster. Book 'em, Danno!

Buster was a good mascot and a fine bearcat, but perhaps his time had come. Thinking back, my high school years (except for my classes with Ms. T and a couple of other great teachers) were a huge waste of time. Would I repeat them? Would I wish them upon my future offspring? Probably not. Will my future children be better off learning from teachers like Colt Atkins and Ms. T than from the slow, droning torture of sitting in Mr. B's classroom? Probably so. That's why I decided to let the Republicrats, the black swan, and your UberUbi device off the hook. Perhaps putting down Buster was really just a mercy killing. Besides, maybe the biggest head-scratcher of all is why a school in central Ohio had a nocturnal, Asian mammal that's neither a cat nor a bear for a mascot in the first place. I mean, seriously, how messed up is that?

Farewell, dear Buster. We hardly knew ye.

Jim Hughes is a starving writer and regular contributor to Slate. *He lives in a three-bedroom, rent-controlled apartment in New York City with five other roommates.*

Reflection Questions

This scenario depicts a world that might be characterized as high-stakes testing and accountability on steroids. For some, this aspect of the scenario may not seem so far-fetched. Readers may be more challenged by or even skeptical about the disruptive influence of technology on the world of education as we know it. We are already witnessing our weekend ritual of standing in line at the video rental store being replaced by having videos delivered to our mailboxes via an online service or downloaded directly to our televisions. Isn't it possible a similar kind of "breathtaking flip" could occur in education?

Below are some questions to help you consider—as an individual or as part of a study group—the implications of this scenario for yourself, your colleagues, your school, and your students.

1   Imagine yourself in this scenario in 2020. You are successful in your profession. What specialized skills, resources, and dispositions did you bring with you from 2010 that contributed to your success? What specialized skills and resources have you acquired to give you an edge in this world of intense, assessment-driven accountability combined with highly competitive, consumer-driven forms of schooling?

2   If you were to see this scenario coming to fruition, what changes might you make in your own professional development or career choices?

3   Think about other education professionals you work with or hire. What skills and resources should they possess in order to be successful in this scenario? What will it take to make sure they retain or acquire these skills and resources by 2020?

4　Think about your school, district, or education organization. Few that exist today appear to survive in this world. Will yours? Will it be sufficiently able to adapt to the changes envisioned in this scenario? What resources will it need to survive and thrive in this future? If this scenario begins to become reality, what changes should your organization begin to make? What should it start doing? What should it *stop* doing?

5　What skills will students need in order to be successful in this scenario? Of those skills, which ones are currently being taught in your setting? Which ones are missing or minimal? What is currently being taught in your setting that would likely be obsolete in the scenario?

6　What will it take to ensure that *every* child is successful? Do you see challenges to the success of every child? What has to happen, starting now and continuing through 2020, for every child to be successful in this scenario?

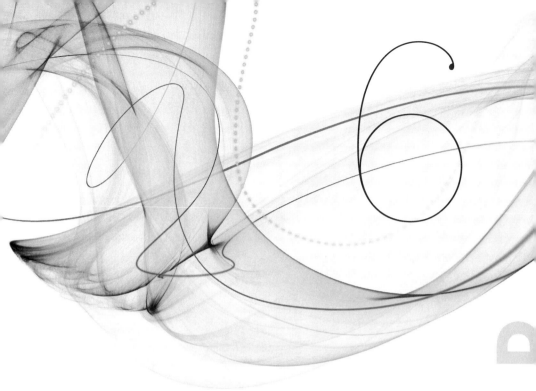

My Path to Juilliard

In this scenario, the system of education has been reinvented, thanks to social networking tools, the economy and changes in consumer habits, and dissatisfaction with traditional K–12 education all culminating in an emerging grassroots revamping of education. Just as Web-based commerce caters to everyone's needs, in this world, parents, students, and society in general have decided that the outcomes of learning should be differentiated according to every child's individual needs and learning goals. Open-source curricula and social networking sites, such as Facebook, Twitter, and Ning, have made it easy for parents and students to form online communities of like-minded people who come together to shape their own educational experiences.

The main character of this scenario is Shana Ling, an eighteen-year-old who has completed an online course of study that has prepared her to enroll in Juilliard's dance academy. The entire scenario is presented as a speech delivered by Shana for a special occasion on the White House lawn.

Deep Causes

Underlying this scenario, which arguably lies the farthest from the world we know today, in the differentiated/reinvented quadrant of our matrix, are several key trends. One of these is continued economic doldrums bringing about a new sense of do-it-yourself self-reliance. At the same time, technology has allowed people to come together in affinity groups, where they can design and provide their own educational experiences. The following sections describe these drivers of change in more detail.

Social Networking

Social networking sites, such as Facebook, Twitter, Ning, Delicious, and LibraryThing, have made it easy to create communities of people based upon common interests. The spontaneous formation of communities around common interests expands the influence of individuals who, before the enabling technologies of social networking, operated as sole agents. Now these individuals can come together, organize, and expand their reach and influence not only to participate in their world, but to help shape it. (For an excellent example of the expanded influence of spontaneously formed communities of like-minded individuals, see Sutter, 2009.)

"My Path to Juilliard" hypothesizes that this trend of self-organizing and shaping one's world according to one's own preferences and affiliations will continue. It is plausible—perhaps even likely—that people will find that it is sufficiently important to shape education according to their own preferences. It is also plausible that, under the right circumstances, this reshaping will bring about change on a scale that will lead to the reinvention of education as we know it.

The Economy and Changes in Consumer Habits

In this scenario, a recession that lasted from 2008 to 2011 has impacted the job market, with surprising effects on education. Due to layoffs, many families have returned to a single-income model. They have downsized their homes (Koch, 2009) and rely more on telecommuting and alternative forms of transportation. More and more companies are hosting webinars or Web conferences rather than having their employees travel. Four-day workweeks have become more common (see Weinschenk, 2008, and Associated Press, 2009b).

In this economic environment, the current system of education is not sustainable. It is simply too expensive to operate schools, to transport students to and from school, and to administer all the myriad aspects of school in its current form. As a result, in this scenario, education funds are turned over to parents in the form of vouchers and tax credits, relieving the educational system of the burden and assigning control of education to parents and students.

Increased Customization

As the scenario unfolds, technology allows people to customize nearly every aspect of their lives. Having a one-size-fits-all form of education has become unacceptable to individuals accustomed to creating and customizing their experiences. The customization of education is facilitated by current technologies, such as Second Life, that provide a virtual world that can be used to organize meetings, lectures, demonstrations, and other means of educating, all of which is further enabled by vouchers and tax credits. Students, parents, and teachers have access to a wealth of information, lessons, and tutorials on sites such as YouTube, PBS, and VoiceThread. Several organizations, including MIT, University of the People, Curriki, CK–12, and OER Commons have released open-source curricula. Larger, more traditional universities and organizations have followed suit, hoping to attract future students and employees.

Students are willing participants in this reshaped, connected world. They prefer to learn in ways that are not found in the typical, traditional school; they prefer random access, graphics before text, and information streaming over the piece-by-piece sharing of expert knowledge by teachers to students (Prensky, 2001). While they use technology to connect with their world, schools demand that they "power down," effectively cutting students off from the tools with which they learn most effectively (Manzo, 2009). The world envisioned in "My Path to Juilliard" is likely very appealing to this generation of learners, to whom connecting, reshaping, and sharing is as natural as breathing.

The open-source education model presented in the scenario complements a current emerging trend around adult learning. We know that, due to prolonged life spans and local and global economies, people are very likely to have multiple careers during their lifetime. When life spans were shorter, people typically completed their education early in life, worked for most of their adult lives, then entered a period of well-deserved leisure toward the end of their lives. Now that we are living well into our nineties and beyond, it makes more sense to break these periods up into cycles so that we study, work, and play several times during our lives (Cahill, Giandrea, & Quinn, 2005; Hiemstra, 1999; U.S. Department of Labor, 2006). The system of education presented in the scenario mirrors graduate and doctoral programs in the 20th century. These programs are almost entirely project-based, with students spending much of their time working with a group or on independent research.

Use of ARRA Stimulus Funds

In this quadrant, it is assumed that the ARRA dollars for education do not have a positive impact on the current system as a whole. Instead, in the scenario, historians compare spending money on the old form of education to throwing millions into the horse-and-buggy industry after it was long apparent that automobiles were the future of transportation.

The use of the stimulus funds to push the current system toward national standards and longer school days turns out to be insufficient to address increasing dropout rates and the demand for real reform. As the educational system continues its heavy reliance on fuel and energy to transport and temporarily house students at designated places of learning (that is, schools), the education establishment's decisions seem grossly out of touch with what is happening in the business world in terms of working from home, using technology to collaborate, and having shorter, not longer, workweeks (Chaddock, 2006; Kingsbury, 2008). Taxpayers, parents, and students become outraged, feeling as though they are forced to put even more time and money into an already-failing system.

ARRA funding is not completely irrelevant in this scenario, however. The scenario does envision an important one-to-one netbook initiative resulting from the stimulus money, which provides robust wireless access in all cities and placates critics of the stimulus program. This ultimately pushes education reform toward reinvention.

The Scenario

The following is a transcript of a keynote speech given by Shana Ling on June 5, 2020, to the first White House Summit on Open-Source Education. At age eighteen, Shana Ling has completed the comprehensive online course of study that she began at age ten, which has prepared her to enroll in the famed Juilliard School. Directed by her parents and herself, Shana Ling's non-school-based education consisted of homeschooling, community-based learning, and online learning options, making significant use of open-source curriculum, social networking learning communities, and other technological innovations. These technologies have made traditional grade-based and building-based schooling obsolete in her world.

Madame President, Fellow Lifelong Learners, Ladies, and Gentlemen: It is such an honor to have been asked to keynote the first White House Summit on Open-Source Education. I represent some of the earliest adopters of a system of education that would have been unfathomable twenty years ago, and I am well aware of how very fortunate I and my peers have been in having the freedom to pursue our interests and dreams and to help to construct our own education.

I know that my learning experience was very different from most of yours. But I believe the fact that I am speaking to you today is recognition of how far the open-source education movement has come since I was a child. I can only hope that it is also an acknowledgment that this sort of approach to learning should be made available to even more students all over the country.

As you know, the lack of personalized instruction and a feeling of disconnection between the classroom and the "real world" led to abysmal dropout rates, with nearly a third of high school students failing to graduate in 2009. My parents tell me that they grew increasingly discouraged at the education I was receiving. Even more distressing to them was helplessly watching as the government continued to pour money from the federal stimulus package into what they saw as a failed system. A critical number of other parents shared similar opinions.

For me, everything changed in the summer of 2013, when I was ten years old. My mother was laid off from her engineering job, and so she had time on her hands. As other well-educated parents also lost jobs, families began rethinking priorities, including their children's education. My parents and a few of their friends decided they could do a better job educating me and their own children themselves.

It has always been interesting to me how much attention I have received because of my education. People always asked me and my mom how we did it. To me, it was as natural as going to the neighborhood school was to others. But I guess we depended much more on technology. We connected with others by sharing websites and book suggestions through resources such as Delicious, Diigo, and LibraryThing. We created communities on Ning, Facebook, Twitter, and Meetup, and shared everything from algebra study advice to setting up science experiments using sites such as YouTube and Google Video.

In other words, we had the technology to communicate and connect with millions of other people who had the same interests as we did, and we had access to any type of information we needed.

Due to my mother losing her job, our family sold our three-bedroom, two-and-a-half-bath house in the suburbs and moved into a community in the Union Station neighborhood of Denver. Our new townhouse had only two bedrooms and smaller dining and living areas. What I liked about it, though, was the fact that I could take the RTD or my bike to any mentor, field trip, or lesson that I needed.

My "classmates" were other students with similar interests and focus areas, not simply other kids who happened to live in the same neighborhood and be in the same grade as I was. As my mother and other parents in the area began creating the informal learning movement, my peers and I became increasingly excited about the fact that we could direct our own learning, use technology tools that we already used socially, and shape our own educational experience. Every time something cool came to the Denver Museum of Nature and Science or to the Denver Art Museum, we were able to co-create an integrated unit that focused on the exhibits. Likewise, if there was construction going on nearby or city planners were meeting to discuss how to solve a particular issue, our parents would organize a way for us to visit the site or listen in on the meeting as a learning opportunity. It was an entirely different way of thinking about schooling. As we got older, my peers and I took even more control of our own schooling—designing units of study, creating grading rubrics together, even taking turns as teachers if someone really had a handle on a subject or skill that others found confusing. Our education resembled the joyful, impromptu learning experiences toward which children are naturally inclined.

While this movement was happening for me and my peers in our urban, middle-class environment, a similar movement was happening in rural and high-poverty, inner-city areas. When my best friend, Chelsea, moved with her family back to her grandparents' ranch in the middle of the Oklahoma panhandle, we not only stayed in touch, we remained classmates. She and her siblings, who found themselves miles from museums, teachers, and other students, used the very tools that we were using to connect and build our own educational experiences to stay connected with us and experience the world. Likewise, a lot of my classmates were inner-city students who wanted a better education than the nearby school could offer. My "classmates" were a very diverse group of students from all over not just Denver or Colorado, but the whole nation—a way more diverse group of kids than I would've learned with had I stayed in my neighborhood school. By this time, the one-to-one netbook distribution and robust citywide wireless installation, made possible by Congress' extension of the stimulus money in 2012, had been completed—effectively closing the digital divide.

By the time I was twelve, across the country, many other parents had also decided that neither public nor independent schools met the needs of their children. The "BIGGEST HOMESCHOOL FACEBOOK GROUP EVER!!!!!!" was 663 members [audience chuckles] strong as early as 2009. Homeschool parents had, by necessity, laid the groundwork for creating informal learning communities. These groups shared lesson plans, linked to videos and other resources, organized field trips within their localities, and invited parents and friends to speak on various subjects. Well-educated, tech-savvy parents began using tools once dismissed as distractions for teenagers to create powerful and well-organized communities. One example of such a group was TwitterMoms, a group of stay-at-home mothers who connected and shared advice, woes, and joys using the popular microblogging site. The group grew exponentially—from just 5,000 members in 2009, when it was mentioned in the popular homemaker's magazine *Redbook* (www .redbookmag.com/kids-family/advice/twitter-moms), to more than 26,000 members in 2010, and a million-plus members a few years later.

A subset of this group, Homeschooling Twitter Moms, began to self-organize sometime in late 2008, focusing on connecting those stay-at-home mothers who were homeschooling their children. We know that even by mid-2010, the group was still small in number (only about 500 members). These women (and a few men) represented former engineers, marketing and communications professionals, educators, artists, actors, dancers, and a variety of other professions. As the economy continued to decline and more and more highly trained professionals were out of work, parents of young children began to question the age-old American dream of doing well in school, going to a prestigious college, and getting a job with the income that would allow for financial freedom. After all, hadn't my parents followed that very prescription, only to find that the careers for which they had prepared were being quickly outsourced to technology or other countries?

Heeding author Daniel H. Pink's (2005) call for creativity and innovation as America's greatest assets, parents began embracing initiatives such as Montessori's and Waldorf's "follow the child" and the Association for Supervision and Curriculum Development's Whole Child initiatives as well as philosophy, arts, dance, and music education. By 2014, the Homeschooling Twitter Moms group had grown to more than one hundred thousand members.

As users were creating their own educational environments, several organizations, such as Curriki, CK–12, MIT, and Insight School, began releasing open-source curricula. Following their example, several nonprofit organizations, colleges and universities, and a few businesses began releasing online curricula and assessments to help students prepare for employment or study at their institution. The acclaimed Juilliard School in New York released a suggested curriculum for K–12 students who hoped to someday study at their academy. The eight universities that make up the Ivy League of colleges released their own K–12 curriculum in late 2012, leaving no uncertainty as to which areas of study students needed to pursue in order to be considered for acceptance. NASA and the National Science Foundation, with funding from the federal government, released high school study plans to prepare students for admission into high-level STEM (science, technology, engineering, and mathematics) fields. Instead of all students following a similar academic path, parents and students were now able to choose a curriculum; organize a community of learners, teachers/mentors, and resources; and have a completely personalized learning experience at a relatively low cost.

My education has completely prepared me for my future career in ballet, thanks to my mentors, technology, and the use of the Juilliard curriculum. My childhood and teen years have been filled with collaborative learning opportunities, both virtual and face to face, that speak directly to my own interests and passions. Whenever I was ready to demonstrate proficiency in any area—be it math, communication, ballet, social studies, or science—I either took an automated test online or found a mentor who had the expertise to assess my learning. As these assessments were gathered and submitted to Juilliard's K–12 academic coordinator, I slowly watched my own progress toward "graduation." I am thrilled to say that I will begin full-time study at the Juilliard School this fall as one of the first students to complete the full curriculum. [Applause.]

Proponents of open-source education tout that our "teachers" are ourselves, guided by professionals with a passion in their content area, and that the concept of teacher burnout is almost nonexistent. Students are able to pursue any area of interest; indeed, "high school dropout" has little meaning in our small but growing community. Technology has made it possible to formatively assess and adjust instruction practically in real time.

However, we know that serious problems still exist. Many argue that children of traditionally blue-collar families are too often encouraged to complete a shorter period of education in order to enter the workforce earlier. A parent whose only career has been working in convenience stores may not know how to search for the resources available to help her child pursue an education in the arts or in the STEM fields. These children very often represent the remaining students who attend traditional, government-funded schools. While these schools have made great strides in terms of childhood health care, one-to-one laptop initiatives, and incentives for professionals to teach in these schools, the education the students receive is far less likely to prepare them for a thriving adulthood than an open-source education would. A pedagogy of poverty still very much exists.

Another area of concern is the fact that world "spikiness" (as opposed to Thomas Friedman's [2007] "flatness," articulated by the likes of Richard Florida [2005]) has the potential to become a reality. Due to complete customization of news resources, RSS feeds, blogs, and podcasts, we have the freedom and ability to listen to and view only the news, topics, and people that interest us. While this allows us to quickly sift through vast amounts of information, personalized news has become a cultural divider among various populations. Now that students have an increasingly customized education, this problem is being exacerbated. Organized communities exist that are focused on beliefs that others find hateful, divisive, and offensive. Forging connections between these various communities has been largely unsuccessful. Recent hacking incidents between religious and secular education groups are a direct result of this trend. As learners, educators, and concerned community members, we have work to do in thinking about how to use technology to bridge these communities so that we ensure a bright future for all.

There have been several recent developments that I think will help to solve these issues. One is the recent addition of life coaches to health and wellness services. Similar to the role of guidance counselors in high schools, these professionals help students to explore their interests, identify and hone their talents, and access learning opportunities. Likewise, recent online initiatives, such as Socratic Method™ and the Purple Brigade, have begun to provide resources to help teachers, parents, and students learn to incorporate peaceful discussion and debate on controversial issues into existing lesson plans. Education continues to evolve and adapt in ever exciting ways, preparing America's citizens for the future.

I thank you for listening. Good night.

Reflection Questions

This scenario depicts a future for education that is, arguably, farthest from the world of education we know today. As a result, of all four scenarios, this one may be the most challenging for readers. Yet one might ask, Is it *impossible* to imagine a parental backlash to standardized outcomes for education, which policymakers view as a sensible means for measuring and increasing the output of public schools but parents see as the exact opposite of what they desire for their own children? Similarly, when one considers the creative destruction that new information technologies have wrought in so many other areas—from entertainment to holiday shopping to graduate education—is it *impossible* to imagine technology transforming K–12 education just as profoundly?

We offer here some questions to help you consider—as an individual or as part of a study group—the implications of this scenario for yourself, your colleagues, your school, and your students.

1   Imagine yourself in this scenario in 2020. You are successful in your profession. What specialized skills, resources, and dispositions did you bring with you from 2010 that contributed to your success? What specialized skills and resources have you acquired to give you an edge in this world of individualized education and highly collaborative, consumer-driven forms of schooling?

2   If you were to see this scenario coming to fruition, what changes might you make in your own professional development or career choices?

3   Think about other education professionals you work with or hire. What skills and resources should they possess in order to be successful in this scenario? What will it take to make sure they retain or acquire these skills and resources by 2020?

4   Think about your school, district, or education organization.
    Few that exist today appear to survive in this world. Will
    yours? Will it be able to adapt to the changes envisioned
    in this scenario? What resources will it need to survive
    and thrive in this future? If you were to see this scenario
    beginning to become reality, what changes should your
    organization begin to make? What should it start doing? What
    should it *stop* doing?

5   What skills will students need in order to be successful in
    this scenario? Of those skills, which ones are currently being
    taught in your setting? Which ones are missing or minimal?
    What is currently being taught in your setting that would
    likely be obsolete in the scenario?

6   What will it take to ensure that *every* child is successful in this
    scenario? Do you see challenges to the success of every child?
    What has to happen, starting now and continuing through
    2020, for every child to be successful in this scenario?

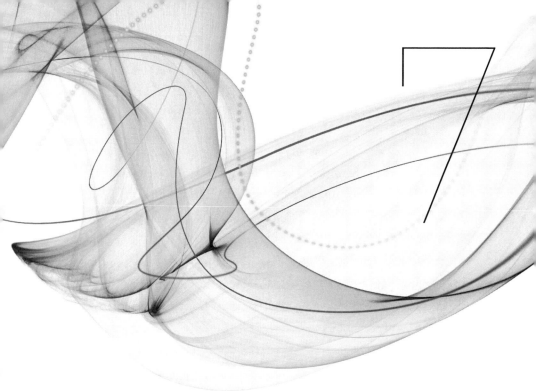

Taking the Next Step

The four scenarios offer very different views of what the future may hold for education. As we've stated earlier, we are *not* suggesting that one of these four alternative futures will definitely occur and that you must pick one, like a pony in a race, and place your bets on it. In reality, the future may look like some combination of these scenarios—or perhaps something entirely different than what we've envisioned here. The point of scenario building—indeed, if it accomplishes nothing else—is to help you develop a voice in the back of your mind that asks, "What if?"

> ✕ What if . . . in an effort to preserve itself, public education will-
> ingly co-opts and incorporates the very reforms it once stoutly
> resisted, transforming into a system relentlessly focused on data,
> individual teacher performance, and helping students succeed on
> high-stakes tests?

✖ What if . . . a backlash develops against the current push for breakthrough innovations and national standards, leaving us with a system similar to the one we have today with one important twist: instead of insisting that every child achieve the same outcomes, it focuses on maximizing the individual learning opportunities for every child?

✖ What if . . . like the faded silhouette of Buster the Bearcat on the exterior of Winesburg High, schools of tomorrow become vague reflections of what they once were, replaced by something akin to drop-in testing and mentoring centers for students who spend most of their time learning at home in front of computers?

✖ What if . . . a do-it-yourself approach to education expands from the one million homeschooled children today to become a larger, nationwide Internet-supported movement to provide every child with unique learning opportunities that tap his or her own unique interests and talents?

Considering these "what ifs" should cause you to wonder, What would *I* do in each of these scenarios? Would I survive? Would I thrive? How would my school or district fare? Would it succeed or fail? Hopefully, like a wedding planner considering the possibility of rain on the wedding day, you will begin to identify some things that you, or your organization, might start to do differently *now*. That, after all, is the purpose of scenario planning: to take different, better informed actions than you might otherwise.

The following sections of this chapter describe how to move from the abstract thought experiment of the scenarios to concrete actions you can take today.

Step 1: Identify Implications

Implications are the conclusions you draw about the meaningful impacts a scenario would have on your organization. They are intellectual assessments of threats, opportunities, and adaptations that might be necessary for your organization to survive and thrive. Implications are *not* actions; for example, "costs are rising" is an implication, while "renegotiate supplier agreements" is an action.

One way to think about the implications of the scenarios for your organization is to complete a SWOT (strengths, weaknesses, opportunities, threats) analysis of each scenario. Begin with any quadrant and imagine that your organization is functioning in this future world. List the strengths and weaknesses of your organization in this scenario. Remember that strengths and weaknesses are *internal* to your organization, whereas threats and opportunities are *external*.

Repeat the SWOT exercise with each of the three other quadrants and then discuss the key implications the process reveals. Are there certain strengths or weaknesses that appear in every quadrant? If so, you may be able to generate ideas for strategic options (in the next step) that will capitalize on your strengths or shore up your weaknesses in many potential futures. With others in your organization, you should brainstorm possible implications for each scenario.

At this stage, it's important that you simply put on the table what this scenario will mean for your organization. It takes some discipline to refrain from leaping to conclusions or proposed actions. Remember, you'll have the opportunity later on to identify proposed actions. So if you haven't already, take the time to answer the reflection questions provided for each scenario, before moving on to step two.

Step 2: Develop Options

Options are the possible actions, strategies, or policies you could undertake today to address the scenario implications. By identifying options in your scenario analysis, you put the scenario to work for your organization.

When you are satisfied with your list of implications, begin to develop options. Start with one scenario, and take the stance that this scenario really *is* the future. List all the things that you could do to prepare for the future. Then list all of the things that you think you *should* do to prepare, including high-level and strategic options. Discuss all the options you've listed, and agree on at least five. Do the same for the other three scenarios.

Once you've finished listing options for each scenario, review your list of about twenty options. Are some options repeated across more than one scenario? If so, these might be areas in which to consider developing robust options, as discussed in chapter 1.

For example, one option you may have listed for all four scenarios is for your organization to become more adept with online learning, providing online courses to students. Similarly, you might have called out an option in several scenarios for integrating standards-based education with individualized curricular pathways—either to prepare for the differentiated world or to ensure that students still receive engaging, meaningful learning experiences in a highly standardized world. This, too, might be a robust option. In both cases, you could take action today to begin to carry out these strategies.

At the same time, it's likely that you may identify some options that are only applicable to one or two scenarios—for example, an option you might identify for the "Buster the Bearcat" scenario would be to turn your school or district into a broadcast center for master teachers, who develop and disseminate lessons to viewers nationwide. This option, however, would be less viable for the two scenarios on the optimized side of the matrix ("Test Day at Bronx City Day School" and "Education to the Max"), where local districts and schools remain the principal providers of education to their own students. Nor would it make as much sense in the open-source curriculum world of "My Path to Juilliard." Thus, this option would be more of a bet-the-farm strategy, something which only works in a single scenario and is thus a higher risk (but has a higher potential payoff if you are correct in your assumptions about the future).

Step 3: Monitor Trends

Now that you've identified actions to take in each scenario, it's important to monitor the extent to which current events appear to be leading to one scenario or another. The process can be as simple as reading newspaper articles and websites through the lens of the scenarios and noting whether they point to a deep cause in one or more of the scenarios. For example, a backlash against standards might suggest the world is heading toward more differentiated outcomes for students. Similarly, a headline about the growing popularity of open-source curricula or online learning could suggest the world is moving toward a more reinvented system of learning. Table 7.1 (pages 126–127) offers some basic indicators that could be used to monitor trends.

A very simple way to track progress would be to check off the boxes for indicators that appear in your scan of the environment and then tally the number of check marks at the bottom of each column. If you find a column with a significantly higher number of check marks than the others, this might suggest the world is moving in the direction of that scenario. Obviously, additional indicators could be identified and tracked, creating a more sophisticated and nuanced way to monitor trends.

Step 4: Take Action

The most important part of scenario planning is, of course, taking action. In order to truly put scenario planning to use, your organization must view monitoring trends and identifying options as an ongoing process. It's important to remain flexible and not become too attached to any particular option. The more fluid you can stay in your assumptions, the better able you will be to weigh evidence about current trends, what the future will bring, and what you can do in response.

In addition, your organization must be poised to change how it does things. People must be comfortable with ambiguity and willing to set aside their own personal desires for the future in order to challenge their assumptions about what may lie ahead. In the final section of this

Table 7.1: Scenario Trends and Indicators to Monitor

Indicators to Monitor	Test Day at Bronx City Day School *standardized / optimized*	Education to the Max *differentiated / optimized*	Who Killed Buster the Bearcat? *standardized / reinvented*	My Path to Juilliard *differentiated / reinvented*
Continued support for standardized outcomes	☐ Strong state support for Common Core standards ☐ Continued political support for data-driven accountability ☐ Creation of sophisticated systems to track and analyze student data		☐ Strong state support for Common Core standards ☐ Continued political support for data-driven accountability ☐ Creation of sophisticated systems to track and analyze student data	
Movement toward differentiated outcomes		☐ States adopting differentiated diplomas ☐ Backlash to Common Core standards ☐ Growth in programs catering to individualized learning (such as career academies and magnet schools)		☐ States adopting differentiated diplomas ☐ Backlash to Common Core standards ☐ Growth in programs catering to individualized learning (such as career academies and magnet schools)

Indicators to Monitor	Test Day at Bronx City Day School *standardized / optimized*	Education to the Max *differentiated / optimized*	Who Killed Buster the Bearcat? *standardized / reinvented*	My Path to Juilliard *differentiated / reinvented*
Support for optimizing the current system	☐ Restoration of education funding to prior levels ☐ Increasing public confidence in the government ☐ Education reform not surfacing as a hot-button political issue	☐ Restoration of education funding to prior levels ☐ Increasing public confidence in the government ☐ Education reform not surfacing as a hot-button political issue		
Movement toward reinvention of the system			☐ More students leaving the system for online learning, homeschooling, and other alternatives ☐ Continued cuts to education funding ☐ Political support for ambitious school reform	☐ More students leaving the system for online learning, homeschooling, and other alternatives ☐ Continued cuts to education funding ☐ Political support for ambitious school reform

book, we provide an example of one school district that has engaged in a scenario-planning process and the benefits they found in using scenarios to think about and plan for an uncertain future.

How Anticipating Change Can Change Everything

In our experience guiding scenario-planning efforts in schools nationwide—from the windswept plains of rural districts in Wyoming to the eight largest, and most urban, districts in the state of Ohio—we have found that when educators use scenario planning to anticipate the future, they come to new insights and take different actions than they would have otherwise through traditional strategic planning methods. To illustrate this point, we'll relate the story of one district we had the privilege of working with for many months, a high-performing district in the Upper Midwest. It had begun to understand that, like the obligatory warning about financial investments, the district's own past performance was no guarantee of its future results.

Kettle Moraine School District is a district of 4,500 students in Wales, Wisconsin (outside Milwaukee), that had long enjoyed a strong tax base, supportive community, and enviable level of student achievement. In 2005, however, like many districts at the time, Kettle Moraine began to encounter funding shortfalls, projecting a multimillion-dollar gap between revenues and expenditures. As the school board and district administrators started looking for ways to reduce spending, they worried that the cuts, if not properly conducted, could undermine the very thing the district most prided itself on: the quality of education it provided to its students.

The more district officials explored the impact of the cuts on education quality, the more they began to ponder exactly what they meant by a *quality* education—especially in light of the rapidly changing world. What would a quality education look like in the future? Would it look different than what it looked like today? Eventually, district leaders decided that they must look beyond short-term concerns about budget cuts and begin to craft a long-term vision for the future of the district (Kettle Moraine School District [KMSD], 2007).

Early on, Kettle Moraine's leaders realized that the district's own history of high performance could be standing in its way. They took to heart the words of Jim Collins (2001), whose book *Good to Great* opens with the lines, "Good is the enemy of great. And that is one of the key reasons why we have so little that becomes great. We don't have great schools, primarily because we have good schools" (p. 1).

The district's leaders decided to seize the moment of budget crises as an opportunity to begin to transform itself into a district that was prepared for, and preparing its students for, the future. For several months, we at McREL had the privilege of working alongside Kettle Moraine and its Transformation Task Force as they developed their own scenarios from scratch around two critical uncertainties: (1) whether the U.S. global economic position would decline or improve over the next ten years and (2) whether the district would be proactive or inactive in response to changes in its external environment.

The district's task force held a series of community forums to gather input from parents, business owners, students, and others in the community. It wrote four scenarios and then reengaged the community in identifying implications and options for each scenario. After sixteen months of hard work, the task force eventually called out four areas as "crucial for the transformation of the Kettle Moraine School District" (KMSD, 2007, p. 6):

1 Developing leaders in the district who move their organizations away from traditional, inflexible, top-down, command-and-control organizations towards those that are more flexible, adaptable, and based on "living systems" theory

2 Creating partnerships with a variety of organizations and businesses in the community, not just for public relations purposes, but to ensure that the district remains attuned to changes happening in the world

3   Incorporating "21st century communication" in all of the district's operations—utilizing the power of informal networks of people, becoming more open and transparent with information, and relying more on electronic and interactive forms of communication

4   Fostering and embracing research and development, first by developing a "strong baseline of accepted practice" throughout the district (KMSD, 2007, p. 49), and then by collecting and analyzing data on those practices to determine if they're working and encouraging new innovations in the district's accepted practices

According to the task force's final report to the community, one person on the team observed, "You know, we probably could have come up with these four categories ten months ago . . . but they would have meant something very different then, than they do now [after engaging in the scenario-planning process]" (KMSD, 2007, p. 6). In short, by helping people in the district and community envision the future, the scenario-planning process created a new urgency for change and innovation that did not previously exist in the district.

"The district sees the need for big change," Kettle Moraine Superintendent Patricia Deklotz told the *Milwaukee Journal Sentinel*, which reported in May 2007 on the district's scenario-planning effort. "We are trying to position ourselves so that we can respond to future challenges in a way that will be proactive rather than reactive. This will be guiding the work that we do for the next five years" (Hetzner, 2007).

Kettle Moraine continues to use the results of the effort to guide its improvement plans. In 2005, the school board directed the district to "transform the educational delivery system to better and more efficiently meet the needs of all students" (KMSD, 2007, p. 8). In response to this charge, Kettle Moraine has developed Global Online Academy of Learning (GOAL), an online high school designed to help students develop 21st century learning skills. Visit www.goalvirtual.com for more information about GOAL. Also available online (www2.kmsd

.edu/ttf/) are the task force's 114-page report, videos made by students as class projects of the four scenarios, and other information.

By engaging in scenario planning, Kettle Moraine was able to avoid the trap many good districts can fall into: becoming complacent and assuming that what made the district effective in the past will make it high-performing in the future. Superintendent Deklotz told her local newspaper, the *Kettle Moraine Index*, "As the task force began to work, we began to understand the only thing certain about the future is change. . . . The only thing we can influence is our response to it" (Haunfelder, 2007).

As its forward-thinking development of a virtual school demonstrates, Kettle Moraine has become proactive as a district, taking bold steps to ensure that when the future arrives, it will be ready for it.

We wish the same thing for you and your organization. We hope this book has challenged your thinking in ways that will help you take actions today that will ensure the success of you and your students in the years to come, whatever the future may bring.

Resources to Keep the Conversation Alive

The conversations, ideas, and stories that are created from the scenarios are of little use to an organization if the discussion does not continue beyond the initial activity. With every news headline, blog article, or tweet that we read, we have an opportunity to reevaluate our guesses of the future, track the progress of our society, and prepare ourselves no matter the future that comes to fruition.

Following is a list of suggested books and reports in six topic areas (economics and innovation, education and the case for change, the influence of generations, globalization and technology, methods, and society and politics), as well as a list of websites and videos that will help to start and keep the conversation going.

Books and Reports

In addition to reading this book, your organization may wish to participate in a jigsaw book study, in which various groups read different books or reports then share what they learned through discussions. Select publications that represent a variety of areas and viewpoints.

Economics and Innovation

Innovation Nation: How America Is Losing Its Innovation Edge, Why It Matters, and What We Can Do to Get It Back by John Kao

Rising to the Challenge: Are High School Graduates Prepared for College and Work? A Study of Recent High School Graduates, College Instructors, and Employers by Peter D. Hart Research Associates

The New Division of Labor: How Computers Are Creating the Next Job Market by Frank Levy and Richard J. Murnane

Wikinomics: How Mass Collaboration Changes Everything by Don Tapscott and Anthony D. Williams

Education and the Case for Change

21st Century Skills, Education & Competitiveness: A Resource and Policy Guide by the Partnership for 21st Century Skills

A Broader, Bolder Approach to Education by the Economic Policy Institute Task Force

America's Perfect Storm: Three Forces Changing Our Nation's Future by Irwin Kirsch, Henry Braun, Kentaro Yamamoto, and Andrew Sum

Crash Course: Imagining a Better Future for Public Education by Chris Whittle

Disrupting Class: How Disruptive Innovation Will Change the Way the World Learns by Clayton M. Christensen, Michael B. Horn, and Curtis W. Johnson

Outliers: The Story of Success by Malcolm Gladwell

Rising Above the Gathering Storm: Energizing and Employing America for a Brighter Economic Future by the National Academy of Sciences, National Academy of Engineering, and Institute of Medicine

Sixteen Trends, Their Profound Impact on Our Future: Implications for Students, Education, Communities, Countries, and the Whole of Society by Gary Marx

The Changing Landscape of American Public Education by Rick Fry

The Future of Educational Entrepreneurship: Possibilities for School Reform by Frederick M. Hess

The Global Achievement Gap: Why Even Our Best Schools Don't Teach the New Survival Skills Our Children Need—And What We Can Do About It by Tony Wagner

Tough Choices or Tough Times: The Report of the New Commission on the Skills of the American Workforce by the National Center on Education and the Economy

Vision 2021: Transformation in Leading, Learning and Community by the National Association of Elementary School Principals

The Influence of Generations

"Digital Natives, Digital Immigrants" by Marc Prensky

Generations: The History of America's Future, 1584 to 2069 by William Strauss and Neil Howe

Learning in the Digital Age by John Seely Brown

Millennial Makeover: MySpace, YouTube, and the Future of American Politics by Morley Winograd and Michael D. Hais

Millennials Rising: The Next Great Generation by Neil Howe and William Strauss

The Coming Generational Storm: What You Need to Know About America's Economic Future by Laurence J. Kotlikoff and Scott Burns

The Empty Cradle: How Falling Birthrates Threaten World Prosperity and What to Do About It by Phillip Longman

The Fourth Turning by William Strauss and Neil Howe

Globalization and Technology

Hot, Flat, and Crowded: Why We Need a Green Revolution—And How It Can Renew America by Thomas Friedman

Nanofuture: What's Next for Nanotechnology by J. Storrs Hall

The Singularity Is Near: When Humans Transcend Biology by Ray Kurzweil

The World Is Flat: A Brief History of the 21st Century by Thomas Friedman

Methods

Foresight, Innovation, and Strategy: Toward a Wiser Future by Cynthia G. Wagner

Get There Early: Sensing the Future to Compete in the Present by Bob Johansen

Inevitable Surprises: Thinking Ahead in a Time of Turbulence by Peter Schwartz

Powerful Times: Rising to the Challenge of Our Uncertain World by Eamonn Kelly

The Art of the Long View: Planning for the Future in an Uncertain World by Peter Schwartz

Society and Politics

A Whole New Mind: Moving From the Information Age to the Conceptual Age by Daniel H. Pink

Collapse: How Societies Choose to Fail or Succeed by Jared Diamond

Crowdsourcing: Why the Power of the Crowd Is Driving the Future of Business by Jeff Howe

Learning for Sustainability by Peter Senge, Joe Laur, Sara Schley, and Bryan Smith

Mapping the Global Future: Report of the National Intelligence Council's 2020 Project by the National Intelligence Council

The Extreme Future: The Top Trends That Will Reshape the World for the Next 5, 10, and 20 Years by James Canton

The Flight of the Creative Class: The New Global Competition for Talent by Richard Florida

The Wisdom of Crowds: Why the Many Are Smarter Than the Few and How Collective Wisdom Shapes Business, Economies, Societies, and Nations by James Surowiecki

Websites

The following websites provide some additional reading and resources for understanding the scenarios and scenario-building process.

www.futureofed.org: KnowledgeWorks Foundation is an Ohio-based nonprofit foundation that has developed its own scenarios for the future, the 2020 Forecast: Creating the Future of Learning. McREL has partnered with the foundation to identify the implications of the KnowledgeWorks scenarios for educators and policymakers.

www.futurist.com: Futurist.com is a website and blog from Glen Hiemstra, a futurist speaker, author, and consultant. His website provides descriptions of many of the trends that underlie our scenarios.

www.gbn.com: McREL uses scenario-planning techniques learned from the Global Business Network (GBN).

www.hsdent.com: The Harry S. Dent Foundation is an economic research and forecasting company that uses its proprietary "Dent Method" to make long-term economic forecasts based on the premise that predictable consumer spending patterns combined with demographic trends foretell economic cycles of growth and decline years or even decades in advance.

www.p21.org: Partnership for 21st Century Skills (P21) is a national organization that advocates for 21st century readiness for every student. It has published a "Framework for 21st Century Learning" that identifies the key skills P21 believes students will need to succeed in a global economy.

Videos

The following videos are excellent conversation starters about looking at the future of education.

A Vision of Students Today by Michael Wesch (www.youtube .com/watch?v=dGCJ46vyR90)

Did You Know? (Shift Happens) by Karl Fisch (http://shifthappens .wikispaces.com)

Future of Education in Campbell County: Four Scenarios for 2016 by McREL (www.mcrel.org/futureofschooling/Scenarios /CCSDScenarioDVDs/tabid/2461/Default.aspx)

Leading the Parade: Transforming Urban Public Education in Ohio by McREL (www.mcrel.org/futureofschooling/Scenarios /Ohio8ScenarioDVDs/tabid/2462/Default.aspx)

The Machine Is Us/ing Us by Michael Wesch (www.youtube .com/watch?v=NLlGopyXT_g)

1990 by Elizabeth Hubbell (http://mcrel.typepad.com/mcrel _blog/2009/04/1990.html)

References and Resources

American Diploma Project. (2004). *Ready or not: Creating a high school diploma that counts.* Washington, DC: Achieve Inc. Accessed at www.achieve.org/files/ADPreport_7.pdf on November 2, 2009.

American Recovery and Reinvestment Act of 2009, H.R. 1, S. 1 111th Congress. (2009). In GovTrack.us (database of federal legislation). Accessed at www.govtrack.us/congress/bill.xpd?bill=s111–1 on October 30, 2009.

Associated Press. (2009a). Duncan gets earful on NCLB "listening tour." *Education Week*, p. 2.

Associated Press. (2009b). Southeastern Louisiana to begin 4-day work week. *WXVT.* Accessed at www.wxvt.com/Global/story .asp?S=10381538&nav=menu1344_2 on June 8, 2010.

Basken, P. (2008, April 18). Electronic portfolios may answer calls for more accountability. *Chronicle of Higher Education*, p. 1.

Batson, A., & Browne, A. (2009, March 13). Wen voices concern over China's U.S. Treasurys. *Wall Street Journal.* Accessed at http://online .wsj.com/article/SB123692233477317069.html on May 14, 2009.

Big Picture Learning. (n.d.). *About us: History.* Accessed at www.bigpicture.org/big-picture-history on October 30, 2009.

Brooks-Gunn, J., & Duncan, G. J. (1997, Summer–Autumn). The effects of poverty on children. *The Future of Children*, 7(2), 55–71.

Buchen, I. H. (2004). *The future of the American school system.* Lanham, MD: ScarecrowEducation.

Bushaw, W. J., & Gallup, A. M. (2008, September). The 40th annual Phi Delta Kappa/Gallup poll of the public's attitudes toward the public schools. *Phi Delta Kappan*, 90(1), 8–20. Accessed at www .pdkmembers.org/members_online/publications/e-GALLUP /kpoll_pdfs/pdkpoll40_2008.pdf on November 2, 2009.

Cahill, K. E., Giandrea, M. D., & Quinn, J. F. (2005). *Are traditional retirements a thing of the past? New evidence on retirement patterns and bridge jobs.* Accessed at www.bls.gov/ore/abstract/ec/ec050100 .htm on June 8, 2010.

Campaign Brief. (2009, May 12). Watch out for Generation Z. Accessed at www.campaignbrief.com/2009/05/watch-out-for-generation-z .html on November 2, 2009.

Canton, J. (2006). *The extreme future: The top trends that will reshape the world for the next 5, 10, and 20 years.* New York: Penguin Group.

Central Intelligence Agency (CIA). (2008). *The world factbook.* Accessed at www.cia.gov/library/publications/the-world-factbook/geos /us.html on July 8, 2010.

Chaddock, G. R. (2006, June 21). US high school dropout rate: high, but how high? *Christian Science Monitor.* Accessed at www.csmonitor .com/2006/0621/p03s02-ussc.html on June 8, 2010.

Christensen, C., Horn, M. B., & Johnson, C. W. (2008). *Disrupting class: How disruptive innovation will change the way the world learns.* New York: McGraw-Hill.

Chudowsky, N., & Chudowsky, V. (2008). *Many states have taken a "backloaded" approach to No Child Left Behind goal of all students scoring "proficient."* Washington, DC: Center on Education Policy.

Coates, J. F., Mahaffie, J. B., & Hines, A. (1997). *2025.* Greensboro, NC: Coates & Jarratt, Inc.

Collins, J. (2001). *Good to great: Why some companies make the leap . . . and others don't.* New York: HarperBusiness.

Conference Board, Inc., Partnership for 21st Century Skills, Corporate Voices for Working Families, & Society for Human Resource Management. (2006). *Are they really ready to work? Employers' perspectives on the basic knowledge and applied skills of new entrants to the 21st century U.S. workforce.* New York: Author. Accessed at www.21stcenturyskills.org/documents/FINAL_REPORT_PDF09 –29–06.pdf on November 2, 2009.

Congress of the United States, Congressional Budget Office (2009, August). *The budget and economic outlook: An update.* Washington, DC: Author. Accessed at www.cbo.gov/ftpdocs/105xx/doc10521/08 –25-BudgetUpdate.pdf on October 24, 2009.

Crooks, E. (2009, June 6). Why your world is about to get a lot smaller [Book review]. *Financial Times.* Accessed at www.ft.com/cms/s/2 /f1395e5e-515f-11de-84c3–00144feabdco.html on September 2, 2009.

Diamond, J. (2005). *Collapse: How societies choose to fail or succeed.* New York: Viking Press.

Dillon, N. (2008, July). The e-volving textbook. *American School Board Journal, 195*(7), 22.

Dychtwald, K. (1999). *Age power: How the 21st century will be ruled by the new old.* New York: Jeremy P. Tarcher/Putnam.

Economic Policy Institute Task Force. (2008). *A broader, bolder approach to education.* Washington, DC: Author. Accessed at www.boldapproach.org on June 9, 2010.

Editorial Board. (2008, August 12). How well are they really doing? [Editorial]. *New York Times*, p. A20. Accessed at www.nytimes .com/2008/08/12/opinion/12tue3.html on May 7, 2009.

Education Commission of the States. (2008a). *Honors/College prep diploma or endorsement.* Accessed at http://mb2.ecs.org/reports /Report.aspx?id=736 on November 2, 2009.

Education Commission of the States. (2008b). *Technical/Vocational diploma or endorsement.* Accessed at http://mb2.ecs.org/reports /Report.aspx?id=738 on November 2, 2009.

Education Week. (2009, June 11). Diplomas count 2009: Broader horizon: The challenge of college readiness for all students. Accessed at www .edweek.org/ew/dc/2009/gradrate_trend.html on July 8, 2010.

Farrell, J. A. (2005, February 27). U.S. deficit builds house of cards. *Denver Post*, p. A29.

Florida, R. (2005). *The flight of the creative class: The new global competition for talent.* New York: HarperCollins Publishers.

Foroohar, R. (2009, June 1). The other "W." *Newsweek.* Accessed at www .newsweek.com/id/199164 on September 2, 2009.

Friedman, T. (2006). *The world is flat: A brief history of the 21st century* (2nd ed.). New York: Farrar, Straus and Giroux.

Friedman, T. (2007). *The world is flat 3.0: A brief history of the 21st century.* New York: Picador.

Friedman, T. (2008). *Hot, flat, and crowded: Why we need a green revolution—and how it can renew America.* New York: Farrar, Straus and Giroux.

Froomkin, D. (2009, May 13). White House watch: The wrong entitlement debate. *Washington Post.* Accessed at http://voices.washingtonpost .com/white-house-watch/the-wrong-entitlement-debate.html on May 14, 2009.

Fry, R. (2006). *The changing landscape of American public education.* Accessed at http://pewhispanic.org/files/reports/72.pdf on March 4, 2008.

Fry, R. (2007, August 30). *The changing racial and ethnic composition of U.S. public schools.* Washington, DC: Pew Hispanic Center.

Fry, R., & Gonzales, F. (2008, August 26). *One-in-five and growing fast: A profile of Hispanic public school students.* Washington, DC: Pew Hispanic Center.

Gardner, H. (1985). *Frames of mind: The theory of multiple intelligences.* New York: Basic Books.

Gladwell, M. (2008). *Outliers: The story of success.* New York: Little, Brown and Co.

Glenn, J. C., & Gordon, T. J. (2005). *2005 state of the future.* Washington, DC: American Council for the United Nations University.

Goldstein, A. (2009, May 13). Alarm sounded on Social Security: Report also warns of Medicare collapse. *Washington Post.* Accessed at www.washingtonpost.com/wp-dyn/content/article/2009/05/12 /AR2009051200252.html on May 14, 2009.

Gonzales, P., Williams, T., Jocelyn, L., Roey, S., Kastberg, D., & Brenwald, S. (2009). *Highlights from TIMSS 2007: Mathematics and science achievement of U.S. fourth- and eighth-grade students in an international context.* Washington, DC: National Center for Education Statistics.

Hall, J. S. (2005). *Nanofuture: What's next for nanotechnology.* Amherst, NY: Prometheus Books.

Haunfelder, K. (2007, May 24). Transformation task force unveils recommendations. *Kettle Moraine Index.* Accessed at www.zwire .com/site/news.cfm?newsid=18380104&BRD=1400&PAG=461&de pt_id=173209 on May 25, 2007.

Hess, F. M. (2008). *The future of educational entrepreneurship: Possibilities for school reform.* Cambridge, MA: Harvard Education Press.

Hetzner, A. (2007, May 25). Kettle Moraine looks at standards: School district wants to stay flexible in a changing world. *Milwaukee Journal Sentinel.* Accessed at www.jsonline.com/story/index.aspx?id=610602 on May 26, 2007.

Hiemstra, G. (1999). Preparing for the 21st century. Accessed at www.futurist.com/archives/futuretrends/preparing-for-the-21st -century on November 2, 2009.

Hoff, D. J. (2009, March 2). National standards gain steam. *Education Week*. Accessed at www.edweek.org//ew/articles/2009/03/04/23nga _ep.h28.html?tkn=YLQFF4uQ8lggHmQMpS8XdGvqZfLaKK1TIMro] on March 10, 2009.

Howe, J. (2008). *Crowdsourcing: Why the power of the crowd is driving the future of business*. New York: Crown Business.

Howe, N., & Nadler, R. (2009, February). Yes we can: The emergence of Millennials as a political generation. Accessed at http://nsc .newamerica.net/publications/policy/yes_we_can on May 8, 2009.

Howe, N., & Strauss, W. (2000). *Millennials rising: The next great generation*. New York: Vintage Books.

Intel, Microsoft, and Cisco Education Task Force. (2008, September 1). *Transforming education: Assessing and teaching the skills needed in the 21st century: A call to action*. Accessed at download.microsoft .com/ . . . /Transformative%20Assessment.pdf on November 2, 2009.

Isaacson, W. (2009, April 19). How to raise the standard in America's schools. *TIME*. Accessed at www.time.com/time/printout /0,8816,1891468,00.html on June 9, 2010.

Jackson, M., with Burdt, C., Bassett, E., & Stein, M. (2004). *The state of the K–12 solutions learning markets & opportunities 2004*. Boston, MA: Eduventures, Inc.

Johansen, B. (2007). *Get there early: Sensing the future to compete in the present*. San Francisco: Berrett-Koehler Publishers, Inc.

Kao, J. (2007). *Innovation nation: How America is losing its innovation edge, why it matters, and what we can do to get it back*. New York: Free Press.

Kelly, E. (2006). *Powerful times: Rising to the challenge of our uncertain world*. Upper Saddle River, NJ: Wharton School Publishing.

Kemple, J. J., & Willner, C. J. (2008). *Career academies: Long-term impacts on labor market outcomes, educational attainment, and transitions to adulthood*. New York: MDRC. Accessed at www.mdrc .org/publications/482/overview.html on November 2, 2009.

Kettle Moraine School District. (2007, May 15). *Transformation education in Kettle Moraine: Recommendations for meeting the needs of all learners. Final report of the school district of Kettle Moraine's Transformation Task Force*. Wales, WI: Author. Accessed at www2 .kmsd.edu/ttf/report.html on July 9, 2010.

Kingsbury, K. (2008, August 14). Four-day school weeks. *TIME*. Accessed at www.time.com/time/magazine/article/0,9171,1832864,00 .html on June 9, 2010.

Kirsch, I., Braun, H., Yamamoto, K., & Sum, A. (2007). *America's perfect storm: Three forces changing our nation's future.* Princeton, NJ: Educational Testing Service.

Klein, A. (2008, August 19). New research center to focus on ed. technology. *Education Week,* p. 1. Accessed at www.edweek.org/ew/artic les/2008/08/19/01techresearch.h28.html?print=1 on November 6, 2009.

Kleiner, A. (2008). *The age of heretics: A history of the radical thinkers who reinvented corporate management* (2nd ed.). San Francisco: Jossey-Bass.

Kling, A. (2009, February). Deficit spending: A scenario analysis. *Cato Institute Tax & Budget Bulletin.* Washington, DC: Cato Institute. Accessed at www.cato.org/pubs/tbb/tbb-54.pdf on April 10, 2009.

Koch, W. (2009, March 17). Americans are moving on up to smaller, smarter homes. *USA TODAY.* Accessed at www.usatoday.com/life /lifestyle/home/2009–03–16-small-homes_N.htm on June 9, 2010.

Kotlikoff, L. J., & Burns, S. (2005). *The coming generational storm: What you need to know about America's economic future.* Cambridge, MA: The MIT Press.

Krugman, P. (2009, February 17). Slumps and spontaneous remission (wonkish) [Blog entry]. Accessed at http://krugman.blogs.nytimes .com/2009/02/17/slumps-and-spontaneous-remission-wonkish on May 7, 2009.

Kurzweil, R. (2005). *The singularity is near: When humans transcend biology.* New York: Penguin Group.

Labaton, S. (2009, September 15). Fed chief says recession is "very likely over." *New York Times.* Accessed at www.nytimes.com/2009/09/16 /business/economy/16bernanke.html?scp=1&sq=%22very%20 likely%20over%22&st=cse on September 16, 2009.

Levy, F., & Murnane, R. J. (2005). *The new division of labor: How computers are creating the next job market.* Princeton, NJ: Princeton University Press.

Longman, P. (2004). *The empty cradle: How falling birthrates threaten world prosperity and what to do about it.* New York: Basic Books.

Los Angeles Unified School District. (2009). *Parent-student handbook 2009–2010.* Los Angeles: Author.

Lynch, M. (2009, August 24). "Peak oil" is a waste of energy. *New York Times.* Accessed at www.nytimes.com/2009/08/25/opinion/25lynch .html?_r=1 on September 2, 2009.

Madland, D., & Logan, A. (2008). *The progressive generation: How young adults think about the economy.* Washington, DC: Center for American Progress. Accessed at www.americanprogress.org /issues/2008/05/progressive_generation.html on November 2, 2009.

Manzo, K. K. (2009, March 30). Students see schools inhibiting their use of new technologies. *Education Week, 28*(27), 10.

Marx, G. (2000). *Ten trends: Educating children for a profoundly different future.* Arlington, VA: Educational Research Service.

Marx, G. (2006). *Sixteen trends, their profound impact on our future: Implications for students, education, communities, countries, and the whole of society.* Alexandria, VA: Educational Research Service.

McCullagh, D. (2009, March 13). If China stops lending us money, look out. *CBS News EconWatch.* Accessed at www.cbsnews.com/blogs /2009/03/13/business/econwatch/entry4864398.shtml on May 14, 2009.

McREL. (2005). *The future of schooling: Educating America in 2014.* Aurora, CO: Author.

Medina, J. (2008). *Brain rules: 12 principles for surviving and thriving at work, home, and school.* Seattle, WA: Pear Press.

Moore, G. E. (1965, April 19). Cramming more components onto integrated circuits. *Electronics, 38*(8). Accessed at http://download .intel.com/museum/Moores_Law/Articles-Press_Releases /Gordon_Moore_1965_Article.pdf on November 2, 2009.

National Academy of Sciences, National Academy of Engineering, and Institute of Medicine. (2007). *Rising above the gathering storm: Energizing and employing America for a brighter economic future.* Washington, DC: National Academies Press. Accessed at www.nap .edu/catalog.php?record_id=11463 on November 2, 2009.

National Association of Elementary School Principals. (2008). *Vision 2021: Transformation in leading, learning and community.* Alexandria, VA: Author.

National Center for Education Statistics. (2008). *Digest of education statistics: 2008.* Washington, DC: U.S. Department of Education Institute of Education Sciences. Accessed at http://nces.ed .gov/programs/digest/d08/index.asp on October 28, 2009.

National Center for Education Statistics. (2009). *NAEP data explorer.* Washington, DC: U.S. Department of Education Institute of Education Sciences. Accessed at http://nces.ed.gov/nationsreportcard /naepdata/ on October 28, 2009.

National Center on Education and the Economy. (2008). *Tough choices or tough times: The report of the New Commission on the Skills of the American Workforce*. San Francisco: Jossey-Bass.

National Commission on Excellence in Education. (1983). *A nation at risk: The imperative for educational reform. A report to the nation and the secretary of education, United States Department of Education*. Washington, DC: Author.

National Intelligence Council. (2004). *Mapping the global future: Report of the National Intelligence Council's 2020 project*. Washington, DC: Author.

National Intelligence Council. (2008). *Global trends 2025: A transformed world*. Washington, DC: Author.

Nelson, C. (2009, July 13). Ten things you didn't know about the Apollo 11 moon landing. *Popular Science*. Accessed at www.popsci.com /military-aviation-amp-space/article/2009–06/40-years-later-ten-things-you-didnt-know-about-apollo-ii-moon-landing on November 2, 2009.

New York City Department of Education. (2009). *Family guide 2009–2010*. New York: Author.

No Child Left Behind Act of 2001, 20 U.S.C. § 6319 (2008).

OASDI Trustees. (2009). *The 2009 annual report of the Board of Trustees of the Federal Old-Age and Survivors Insurance and Federal Disability Insurance Trust Funds*. Washington, DC: Author. Accessed at www.socialsecurity.gov/OACT/TR/2009/tr09.pdf on July 12, 2010.

Odden, A., Monk, D., Nakib, Y., & Picus, L. (1995). The story of the education dollar: No academy awards and no fiscal smoking guns. *Phi Delta Kappan, 77*(2), 161–68.

Ogilvy, J., & Schwartz, P. (n.d.). *Plotting your scenarios*. San Francisco: Global Business Network. Accessed at www.gbn.com/articles/pdfs /gbn_Plotting%20Scenarios%20new.pdf on July 12, 2010.

Olson, L. (2007, April 18). Gaps in proficiency levels on state tests and NAEP found to grow. *Education Week, 26*(33), 12.

Organisation for Economic Co-operation and Development. (2008). *Education at a glance 2008: OECD indicators*. Paris: Author.

Orman, S. (2008). *Suze Orman's 2009 action plan: Keeping your money safe & sound*. New York: Spiegel & Grau.

Partnership for 21st Century Skills. (2008). *21st century skills, education & competitiveness: A resource and policy guide*. Tucson, AZ: Author.

Peter D. Hart Research Associates. (2005, February). *Rising to the challenge: Are high school graduates prepared for college and work? A study of recent high school graduates, college instructors, and employers.* Washington, DC: Author.

Pink, D. H. (2001). *Free agent nation: The future of working for yourself.* New York: Warner Business Books.

Pink, D. H. (2005). *A whole new mind: Moving from the information age to the conceptual age.* New York: Riverhead Books.

Prensky, M. (2001, September/October). Digital natives, digital immigrants. *On the Horizon, 9*(5), 1–6. Accessed at www.marcprensky .com/writing/Prensky%20-%20Digital%20Natives,%20Digital%20 Immigrants%20-%20Part1.pdf on February 27, 2008.

Race to the Top Fund, RIN 1810-AB07, 55 Fed. Reg. 74, 144 (July 29, 2009).

Reuters. (2009, October 22). Reducing deficit key to US rating: Moody's. Accessed at www.cnbc.com/id/33426521 on October 24, 2009.

Rivlin, A. M. (2009, January 21). Testimony given to the Senate Budget Committee at the Brookings Institution and Georgetown University. Accessed at http://budget.senate.gov/democratic/testimony/2009 /Rivlin-1–21-testimony.pdf on May 7, 2009.

Rubin, J. (2009). *Why your world is about to get a whole lot smaller: Oil and the end of globalization.* New York: Random House.

Schein, E. H., with DeLisi, P. H., Kampas, P. J., & Sonduck, M. M. (2003). *DEC is dead, long live DEC: The lasting legacy of Digital Equipment Corporation.* San Francisco: Berrett-Koehler Publishers, Inc.

Schwartz, P. (1991). *The art of the long view: Planning for the future in an uncertain world.* New York: Doubleday.

Schwartz, P. (2003). *Inevitable surprises: Thinking ahead in a time of turbulence.* New York: Gotham Books.

Seely Brown, J. (2004). *Learning in the digital age.* Accessed at www .johnseelybrown.com/learning_in_digital_age-aspen.pdf on March 5, 2008.

Senge, P., Laur, J., Schley, S., & Smith, B. (2006). *Learning for sustainability.* Cambridge, MA: Society for Organizational Learning, Inc.

Social Security Administration. (2009, August 5). *Social security basic facts.* Washington, DC: Author. Accessed at www.socialsecurity.gov /pressoffice/basicfact.htm on July 14, 2010.

Social Technologies. (2007, September). New jobs for 2020. *Change Waves*. Accessed at www.socialtechnologies.com/FileView.aspx ?filename=ChangeWaves Sept2007.pdf on June 7, 2010.

Stempel, J. (2009, February 28). Buffett says U.S. Treasury bubble one for the ages. Reuters. Accessed at http://uk.reuters.com/article /businessNews/idUKTRE51R1Q720090228?sp=true on April 10, 2009.

Stengel, R. (2009, April 15). Arne Duncan: The apostle of reform. *TIME*, *173*(16), 37. Accessed at www.time.com/time/politics/article /0,8599,1891473,00.html on November 2, 2009.

Stevenson, K. R. (2006). *Educational facilities within the context of a changing 21st century America*. Washington, DC: National Clearinghouse for Educational Facilities.

Strauss, W., & Howe, N. (1991). *Generations: The history of America's future, 1584 to 2069*. New York: Quill William Morrow.

Strauss, W., & Howe, N. (1997). *The fourth turning: An American prophecy. What the cycles of history tell us about America's next rendezvous with destiny*. New York: Broadway Books.

Strauss, W., & Howe, N. (2001, October 29). Sept. 11 tragedy marks another turning point. *USA TODAY*. Accessed at www.lifecourse .com/media/articles/lib/2001/102901-ut.html on September 2, 2009.

Surowiecki, J. (2004). *The wisdom of crowds: Why the many are smarter than the few and how collective wisdom shapes business, economies, societies, and nations*. New York: Doubleday.

Sutter, J. D. (2009, May 4). Backyard scientists use Web to catalog species, aid research. CNN.com. Accessed at www.cnn.com/2009 /TECH/science/05/04/citizen.science.climate.change/index.html?iref =t2test_techmon on June 9, 2010.

Svaldi, A. (2010, July 11). Road to recovery long, slow. *Denver Post*, pp. 1K, 8K.

Taleb, N. N. (2007). *The black swan: The impact of the highly improbable*. New York: Random House.

Tapscott, D., & Williams, A. D. (2008). *Wikinomics: How mass collaboration changes everything* (2nd ed.). New York: Penguin Group.

TIME. (1998, April 13). *TIME 100: 1900 vs. now*. Accessed at http://205.188.238.109/time/time100/timewarp/timewarp_us.html# on July 11, 2010.

Toch, T. (2006). *Margins of error: The education testing industry in the No Child Left Behind era*. Washington, DC: Education Sector.

Trotter, A. (2008, March 21). Software industry promotes goals for school technology. *Education Week.* Accessed at www.edweek.org/ew /articles/2008/03/26/29vision.h27.html?print=1 on November 2, 2009.

U.S. Census Bureau. (n.d. *a*). *U.S. POPClock projection.* Accessed at www.census.gov/population/www/popclockus.html on July 8, 2010.

U.S. Census Bureau. (n.d. *b*). *Population profile of the United States: National population projections.* Accessed at www.census.gov /population/www/pop-profile/natproj.html on October 29, 2009.

U.S. Census Bureau. (2004). U.S. cell phone use up more than 300 percent, statistical abstract reports [Press release]. *Nation's Data Book.* Accessed at www.census.gov/Press-Release/www/releases/archives /miscellaneous/003136.html on July 1, 2009.

U.S. Census Bureau. (2007). Information and communications. *Statistical abstract of the United States: 2007.* Table 1132, p. 720. Accessed at www.census.gov/prod/2006pubs/07statab/infocomm.pdf on November 2, 2009.

U.S. Census Bureau. (2008, August 14). An older and more diverse nation by midcentury [Press release]. Accessed at www.census.gov /Press-Release/www/releases/archives/population/012496.html on July 1, 2009.

U.S. Census Bureau. (2009). *The 2009 statistical abstract: The national data book.* Accessed at www.census.gov/compendia/statab/cats /births_deaths_marriages_divorces/life_expectancy.html on October 29, 2009.

U.S. Department of Education. (2004). *National education technology plan.* Washington, DC: Author. Accessed at www.ed.gov/about/offices /list/os/technology/plan/2004/site/edlite-default.html on June 9, 2010.

U.S. Department of Education. (2009a). *State fiscal stabilization fund.* Accessed at www.ed.gov/policy/gen/leg/recovery/factsheet /stabilization-fund.html on August 28, 2009.

U.S. Department of Education. (2009b). *Department of Education progress report.* Accessed at www.ed.gov/about/reports/annual/100days .html on May 6, 2009.

U.S. Department of Education. (2009c). Race to the Top Fund: Notice of proposed priorities, requirements, definitions, and selection criteria. Accessed at www.ed.gov/legislation/FedRegister/proprule/2009–3 /072909d.html on November 2, 2009.

U.S. Department of Education. (2009d). Investing in Innovation Fund (i3): Notice of proposed priorities, requirements, definitions, and selection criteria. Accessed at www.ed.gov/legislation/FedRegister /proprule/2009–4/100909a.html on October 30, 2009.

U.S. Department of Education, Office of Elementary and Secondary Education. (2009, April). *Guidance: Funds under Title I, Part A of the Elementary and Secondary Education Act of 1965. Made available under the American Recovery and Reinvestment Act of 2009.* Accessed at www.ed.gov/policy/gen/leg/recovery/guidance/title-i.pdf on October 28, 2009.

U.S. Department of Labor, Bureau of Labor Statistics. (2006, August 25). *Number of jobs held, labor market activity, and earnings growth among the youngest Baby Boomers: Results from a longitudinal survey.* USDL 06–1496. Washington, DC: Author.

Wagner, C. G. (2005). *Foresight, innovation, and strategy: Toward a wiser future.* Bethesda, MD: World Future Society.

Wagner, T. (2008). *The global achievement gap: Why even our best schools don't teach the new survival skills our children need—and what we can do about it.* New York: Basic Books.

Walker, D. (2009, May 12). America's triple A rating is at risk. *Financial Times.* Accessed at www.ft.com/cms/s/0/5534bd04–3f27–11de-ae4f -00144feabdco.html?nclick_check=1 on May 14, 2009.

Weick, K. E., & Sutcliffe, K. M. (2001). *Managing the unexpected: Assuring high performance in an age of complexity.* San Francisco: Jossey-Bass.

Weinschenk, C. (2008, July 2). Telecommuting thrives, as part of the bigger picture. *IT Business Edge.* Accessed at www.itbusinessedge .com/cm/community/features/interviews/blog/telecommuting -thrives-as-part-of-the-bigger-picture/?cs=23017 on June 9, 2010.

Whittle, C. (2005). *Crash course: Imagining a better future for public education.* New York: Riverhead Books.

Winograd, M., & Hais, M. D. (2008). *Millennial makeover: MySpace, YouTube, and the future of American politics.* New Brunswick, NJ: Rutgers University Press.

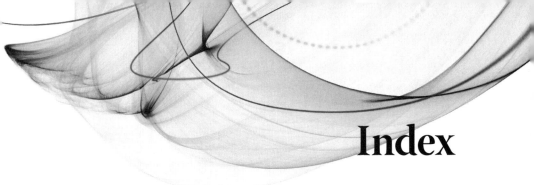

Index

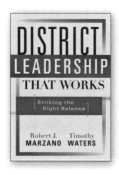

District Leadership That Works
By Robert J. Marzano and Timothy Waters
Learn how to create district-defined goals while giving building-level staff the stylistic freedom to respond quickly and effectively to student failure.
BKF314

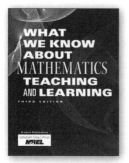

What We Know About Mathematics Teaching and Learning
By McREL
Designed for accessibility, this book supports mathematics education reform and brings the rich world of education research and practice to preK–12 educators.
BKF395

21st Century Skills
Edited by James Bellanca and Ron Brandt
Education luminaries reveal why 21st century skills are necessary, which skills are most important, and how to help schools include them in curriculum and instruction.
BKF389

Mind, Brain, & Education
Edited by David A. Sousa
Understanding how the brain learns helps teachers do their jobs more effectively. In this book, primary researchers share the latest findings in neuroscience, as well as applications, examples, and innovative strategies.
BKF358

Solution Tree | Press

a division of
Solution Tree

Visit solution-tree.com or call 800.733.6786 to order.

Solution Tree | Press

a division of

Solution Tree

Solution Tree's mission is to advance the work of our authors. By working with the best researchers and educators worldwide, we strive to be the premier provider of innovative publishing, in-demand events, and inspired professional development designed to transform education to ensure that all students learn.

Based in Denver, Colorado, McREL (Mid-continent Research for Education and Learning) is a nonprofit organization dedicated to its mission of making a difference in the quality of education and learning for all through excellence in applied research, product development, and service. For more than forty years, McREL has served as the federally funded regional educational laboratory for seven states in the U.S. heartland. Today, it provides services to an international audience of educators. To learn more about McREL's services or how we can help you apply guidance from this book in your organization, contact McREL at 1.800.781.0156 or info@mcrel.org.